VIRTUE IS ITS OWN PUNISHMENT

VIRTUE IS ITS OWN PUNISHMENT

A MEMOIR OF GROWING UP MORMON

BY

RICHARD MENZIES

New University Press LLC

Los Angeles • Las Vegas

A Mormon classroom. Photograph by Richard Menzies

***

Author's Note:

This book is a literary account of the author's youth and spiritual journey. The characters depicted are real. Many of their names have been changed to protect the innocent and guilty alike.

Copyright © 2014 by Richard Menzies

All rights reserved
No part of this book may be used or reproduced in any fashion without permission, except for brief quotations embodied in critical articles or reviews.

Printed in the United States of America
First Edition

Cover by Trescela Samson, adapted from a photograph by the author

For information about permission to reproduce selections from this book, contact:
www.newuniversitypress.com

ISBN: 9780982921937

Library of Congress Control Number: 2013952877

> **"THE NEIGHBOR THINKS; THEREFORE, I AM."**
> -*Hippocrates*

> **"BUT WHAT WILL YOU DO WITHOUT FREEDOM?"**
> -William Wallace, Martyred Scottish Rebel

Table of Contents

	Preface	9
1	The Hierarchy of Heaven	11
2	Jesus Wants Me for a Something	25
3	Not-So-Fast Times at Warren G. Harding Elementary	36
4	Going Down for the Count	43
5	All Work and No Pay at the Deseret News	48
6	The Least You Can Be Is a Saint	64
7	Missing In Action? Not Me!	75
8	At Play in the Beet Fields of the Lord	83
9	There's a Place in France	93
10	A Marvelous Work and Wonder Bread	102
11	Hawaii Calls, and I Pick Up	111
12	Redeeming the Dead, Transporting the Undead	117
13	Whither Thou Goest, Mimsy Farmer, I Shall Follow	124

14	Bishop Snarr Turns Up the Heat	136
15	Onward Stripling Warriors	140
16	The Importance of Being Like Ernest	146
17	Dwight Weed Goes Missing	158
18	Encountering an Actual Educator and a Hot Coed	163
19	Driven to Drink by a Scarlett Letter	175
20	A Light at the End of the Funnel?	185
21	Sounds of Silence vs. Sound of Music	196
22	I Have a Dream	200

Preface

Whenever I move into a new place, I'm not there long before two young men wearing narrow neckties, white shirts and dark suits come knocking at my door. I don't have to read their plastic name tags to know who they are; they're Mormons, come to welcome me into "the ward."

A Mormon ward is akin to a parish, a congregation, a flock. Should a member stray from his flock and wander off to some remote corner of the planet, he can rest assured the folks back home are hot on his trail. And chances are good they'll find him, thanks to a vast network of undercover informants—not to mention billions of files the church keeps in a climate-controlled, atomic bombproof vault buried deep underneath the granite walls of Little Cottonwood Canyon. There you will find a dossier on each and every baptized Mormon, living or dead—including members like me, who have gone AWOL.

"Hi, there," chirps the slightly older-looking of the pubescent pair. "I'm Elder Jensen and this is Elder Jones. We understand you just moved into our ward."

Hopeful grins fixed on their cleanly shaven faces, the two project an air of boundless optimism. However, I also catch a faint whiff of apprehension, a fear that theirs might be a mission impossible.

What to make of this renegade, who according to his file, was at one time not merely an active member of the church but an exemplary one? Born on April 6, the same day the church was founded, ordained an elder at the age of nineteen. A graduate of Brigham Young University! As a boy, he collected more perfect attendance pins than anyone in the history of the

Carbondale First Ward. The Audie Murphy of attendance!

So what the hell went wrong?

It's a question that weighs heavily on the minds of elders Jensen and Jones, and one that I'd dearly love to answer if only they would ask. But given the precious little interest they actually have in me as a person, *why* should they ask? If *only* they *cared* how I am, if *only* I were anything to them other than just another name on their to-do list. If *only* they wanted something from me other than total capitulation—what a pleasant chat we could have then! Because, even as I shut the door on their bright sunny faces, it occurs to me that what I have to say about my life as a Mormon could easily fill a book.

CHAPTER ONE

THE HIERARCHY OF HEAVEN

According to Mormon theology, each and every one of us existed long before we were conceived in the womb. We existed as spirits in heaven, where nothing unpleasant ever happens. We were one big happy family and everyone was perfectly content and satisfied—that is, except for our Heavenly Father. Heavenly Father wasn't satisfied because what with no trials to endure, no obstacles to overcome, no challenges to meet, it was impossible for Him to know which of His children were worthy of his love and which were not. So He devised a plan whereby each of His children would be sent away to earth camp for a period of approximately three score and ten years. There we would undergo a battery of tests and temptations in order to determine whether we are indeed worthy of dwelling in His House forever.

Those who fail the test will not be allowed back in. Those who pass—but only barely—will be assigned to quarters on the ground floor, a level of glory known as the *Telestial Kingdom.*

Just above the Telestial Kingdom lies the *Terrestrial Kingdom,* a more exalted neighborhood reserved for those who come home with a decent report card. Accommodations there are nice, but not nearly as nice as those enjoyed by residents of the *Celestial Kingdom,* a heavenly penthouse suite reserved for those who graduate *summa cum laude.* Once you have made it into the Celestial Kingdom, you need never take another test, ever again.

Because earth isn't nearly as capacious as heaven, not all of God's children can be sent away to earth camp at once; thus the waiting period may run into hundreds, even thousands of years. But no matter, for a century on earth amounts to no more than an eye blink in heaven. Thus one minute you may find yourself standing in a long line of untested spirit children, some attired in business suits, others in animal skins. A minute or so passes and you find yourself at the front of the line, facing a gilded hatch marked EXIT.

The door swings open and out you go like an obedient paratrooper. It's not entirely a blind leap of faith, however, for before you jump you are permitted to choose your earthly mother and father. Which is why, say the Mormons, children generally resemble their parents—because in the pre-existence they picked them out of a line-up!

What isn't so clear is why some earthly parents are chosen. What boy in his right mind would look down upon a sea of hairy heads and point to a bald one? What daughter would choose, say, Joan Crawford over Julie Andrews? Who, given a choice, would choose a dank hovel in Bangladesh over a luxury mansion in Brentwood? And why, during the darkest days of World War II, would anyone choose to be conceived in Poland?

I put the question to my wife, whose Jewish mother passed the nine months prior to her daughter's birth alternately hiding from Nazi storm troopers and dodging Allied bombs.

"Frankly, Anne, I don't understand what possessed you to undertake such a terrible risk. Why didn't you choose to be born in Utah like I did?" And by Utah I mean the Western American state—not the blood-soaked beach in Normandy.

Anne didn't even look up from her book. Unlike women brought up behind the Zion curtain, her mind isn't a rat's maze of theological conundrums.

I remember the day back in 1978 when church president Spencer W. Kimball abolished the church's long-standing policy prohibiting men of African descent from holding the priesthood. In Utah, the announcement was heralded as proof positive that God does indeed continue to speak to his children through a living prophet.

But how is it, I wondered aloud, that eternal verities must constantly be upgraded and revised? If blacks are worthy of holding the priesthood today, then how is it that only yesterday—much less than an eye blink, celestial time—they were not? Is it possible that somehow God made a mistake?

"Why not?" replied Anne, still not looking up from her book. "After all, He's only human."

* * *

According to my birth certificate, I came to earth on the sixth day of April, 1943. I was born at the old St. Mark's hospital on Beck Street in Salt Lake City, across the road from a gravel pit and downwind from an oil refinery. Clearly my parents were hoping for a daughter, and had given no thought whatever as to what they might name me, should I turn out to be still another son. Hence I was logged in, simply, as "Baby Boy Menzies."

A few days afterward mother and son went home to a stucco house on Redondo Avenue, a stone's throw from Sugarhouse Park—which at the time wasn't a park but the Utah state prison. It was a most pleasant time of year, with daffodils and forsythia in bloom, the aroma of awakening grass in the air. The war in Europe was far, far away; the only gunfire heard in the Sugarhouse district was an occasional volley at dawn from inside the walls of the penitentiary, signifying that some condemned felon had faced a firing squad for his crime.

My father worked as a schoolteacher; Mom was a housewife. By the time I entered the picture they'd already been together eight years and had spawned two other sons: James, six, and Chuck, three.

Had my family stayed put on Redondo Avenue, mine might very well have been just another typical Mormon boyhood in a white and delightsome neighborhood of leafy streets, tidy brick homes, multiple ice cream shops and ward houses. Most likely I'd have graduated from Highland High School and served a two-year mission for the church. Six months after returning, I'd have married a girl from my ward and embarked on a conventional, white-collar career. By now Sherilyn and I would be the parents of six flaxen-haired, blue-eyed children: Nephi, JereLyn, Spencer, Orrin, Cloyd, and Cloydene.

But we didn't stay put. In 1944 my father took a job with the Grazing Service, a precursor to the Bureau of Land Management, which required a transfer to the cultural hinterlands. My mother bade a tearful farewell to her Sugarhouse friends and neighbors, more than a few of whom expressed deep misgivings. Nor did our family's exodus from Zion sit particularly well with my parents' kinfolk, many of whom were comfortably settled in verdant Utah County, also known as the *holy land*.

Carbon County, by contrast, has long been considered the bastard province of the intermountain Mormon empire. Situated seventy miles south and east of the aforesaid holy land, on the back side of the Wasatch Plateau, her rough-and-tumble coal camps hadn't been settled by religious zealots—rather, by a hodgepodge of immigrants from Italy, Greece, Slovenia, Mexico, Scotland, Ireland, Wales, and Japan. They came seeking not salvation in the next world but gainful employment in this one.

Liquor had always flowed freely in Carbon County, even during Prohibition. Gambling dens and houses of prostitution were firmly entrenched, as were labor unions and the Democratic Party. Visitations from members of the ruling gerontocracy of the LDS church—so-called *general authorities* are exceedingly rare, and it's generally thought more likely the devil will open a coal mine there than the saints will ever build a temple.

For a time our family camped in a flophouse on the wrong side of the railroad tracks in south Carbondale—until one day Dad spotted a FOR RENT sign on a tiny house on Carbon Avenue, a dwelling destined to become enshrined in our family's oral history as "The Little House."

The most memorable thing about The Little House was that it stood within twenty feet of an irrigation canal that had evidently claimed the life of every unattended toddler who had ever ventured near it. Determined that hers would be the first to escape the curse, Mom filled my head with stories of red-eyed monsters and slavering serpents that lurked just beneath the murky surface—vicious creatures with long tentacles whose principal food source was two-year-old boys.

Mom's strategy worked. Not only did I never go near the water, I became so hydrophobic that all it took was a raindrop to a plunge me into the highly agitated state known in those days as "a conniption fit."

One day when I was about three years old, Dad showed up behind the wheel of a huge flatbed truck. "Grab your stuff," he announced. "We're moving."

It took all of five minutes to load all our belongings. Then away on our mattresses we went, like Joads bound for California, except that we didn't go all the way to California but just seven city blocks, to our new home, "The Big House."

By today's standards, The Big House wasn't all that big—only five rooms and one bath—but to my mother it looked like San Simeon. For the first time in their married life, my parents had a room separate from their kids. As for the boys—well, instead of being stacked one atop the other like cordwood, now we could sleep side by side—like enchiladas.

The best part about The Big House was that it had a full basement, several hundred square feet of undeveloped floor space just begging to be framed up and subdivided into separate dark cubicles. In time there would be two more bedrooms, a laundry room for Mom, a workshop for Dad, and of course the furnace room and coal bin.

The back yard was spacious, fenced, and didn't border upon an irrigation canal teeming with boy-eating aquatic life. There was a one-car garage, and—will wonders never cease—a clothesline. Mom was beside herself with joy. Many's the time in years to come she would look back upon the day we moved into The Big House as the happiest of her entire life.

It was good she liked it, because in those days taking out a thirty-year mortgage was a commitment akin to selecting a burial plot. Once you moved in, you were expected to stay put. You stayed until the mortgage was paid off. You stayed until the kids had all grown up and moved away, and until the family dog had died of old age. Then you stayed some more, until finally the county coroner came to cart you off. Even today I can walk the streets of my home town and recite the name of each and every permanently installed family in each and every house—even though the monograms on the aluminum storm doors have been changed.

We lived on what was at that time the northern fringe of Carbondale, surrounded by neighbors who had all arrived about the same time we did—shortly after the end of World War II. Many of the local men were veterans of that conflict, including the father of my very first friend, Terry.

Terry lived a block away in a minuscule rental that was even smaller than The Little House. His mother, I remember, looked a lot like Betty Grable and indulged in an art form known as "pastels." Terry's father drove a dump truck at a local coal mine. As I vividly recall, he worked the *graveyard* shift as a member of a *skeleton crew*. I still get shivers just thinking about it.

Each morning just after dawn, Terry's dad would return from the mine coated head to toe with coal dust—everything black except for the whites of his eyes and gleaming teeth. When he spied his son, he'd grin broadly and reach out with loving arms. Terry would scream and pitch a conniption fit.

Since his father slept during the day, the two of us were obliged to play outside. We'd hang out in the alley that ran between our houses, foraging for wild raspberries and sometimes helping ourselves to Old Lady Fox's not-so-wild apricots. At other times we'd spend hours climbing up and down the sides of Terry's father's dump truck. If we were packing cap pistols, we'd pretend to be cowboys, and inevitably an argument would break out over which of us would get top billing.

"Let's play cowboys," Terry would announce. "I'll be Roy Rogers; you be Gene Autry."

"You can't be Roy Rogers," I'd protest. "You were Roy Rogers yesterday."

"Doesn't matter. I chose first. You have to be Gene Autry."

"Dammit, I don't wanna be Gene Autry! I wanna be *King of the Cowboys!*"

Off we'd go, me stuck on Autry's horse *Champion*, while Terry galloped ahead astride the incomparable palomino *Trigger*. Beside me rode an imaginary Pat

Buttram, no match for Roy's humorous sidekick Gabby Hayes. No matter that Terry was obliged to share a bed with Dale Evans, I still complained bitterly.

Then one day Terry announced that he was tired of quarreling. We could *both* be Roy Rogers, he said.

"What are you saying, Terry?" I asked. "How can we *both* be Roy Rogers?"

"Why not? Anything's possible in the world of make-believe. 'When you wish upon a star, makes no difference who you are.'"

With that, Terry commenced climbing up the side of his father's dump truck, except that in his mind's eye it wasn't a dump truck, but one of those bullet-pocked granite boulders in the Alabama Hills. I started climbing up the opposite side.

"What's the story line?" I asked.

"We're climbing up this big cliff, see, and it's about a thousand feet straight down to the bottom of a box canyon. You don't see me just yet, but when you do, you try to bushwhack me."

"*I* bushwhack *you*? Roy Rogers would never bushwhack anybody."

"Just do as I say."

At the top of the dump truck, I saw Terry's head pop into view. I drew aim with my cap pistol and fired. Terry fired back; I fired again.

"Hey, I shot you," he shouted. "You're supposed to fall."

"*You* shot *me*? I shot you first."

"You shot *at* me, but you didn't *hit* me. You only grazed me. I'm Roy Rogers, remember?"

"Well, so am I. So how do you figure I could have missed you?"

"Because Roy Rogers would never ..."—and here I could sense that my friend had ventured a bit beyond his depth in the cosmological waters of make-believe—"because Roy Rogers would never ... commit suicide."

The argument ended abruptly when I lost my footing and fell, one thousand feet straight down onto Terry's graveled driveway. When I came to, I discovered I had lacerated my forearm—a wound that would result in a scar that I carry to this day. Unfortunately, I've never felt comfortable talking about it:

"Oh, *this*? Well, once I was Roy Rogers, see, and I fell off a dump truck."

When Terry and I weren't bickering over such things as horses, dogs, and humorous sidekicks, we quarreled over who was the world's greatest singer. The candidates, as I recall, were Bing Crosby, Frank Sinatra, Mario Lanza and Johnny Ray. But since none of the above had been crowned King of the Crooners, it was impossible for us to know for sure which of them was the greatest. Moreover, it's hard to imagine an interesting game that would involve Mario Lanza, Johnny Ray and a dump truck. However, if the capacity to burst into tears at any moment counted for anything, I suppose I'd have wound up playing the part of Johnny Ray.

Before he became a "skeleton," working the graveyard shift, Terry's father had fought the Japanese in the Pacific Theater. According to Terry, his dad was braver than G.I. Joe and Combat Kelly combined. One of the souvenirs Terry's father had brought home from the battlefield was an elaborately decorated samurai sword—the very sword, according to Terry, that

Hirohito had surrendered to General MacArthur aboard the battleship Missouri. Nighttimes, it occupied a place of honor on the wall above his parents' sofa; during the day it played a major role in an ongoing pirate fantasy Terry and I had cooked up.

Whenever his mother wasn't looking we'd take down the sword and haul it off to nearby Wood Hill. There we'd place it on the ground and cover it over with rocks. Then we'd turn our backs and step off a certain number of paces—what we figured was the approximate distance between Spain and Nova Scotia.

By and by, two little heads would appear on the far horizon, eyes glued to the ground as we retraced our footsteps back to the buried treasure.

"Avast, matey! Thar be the rock pile I remember from ten minutes ago."

"Awrrr. Shiver me timbers, lad. Thar she be!"

Whereupon the two of us would drop to our knees and begin to burrow. Hirohito's sword would enjoy a brief moment in the sun, only to be reburied. Each time we chose a different hiding spot, hoping to find just the right hiding spot—until one day we found such a good hiding spot that when we returned, we found *nothing*! All that afternoon we searched, leaving hardly a stone on Wood Hill unturned. The search resumed early the next day and continued into the next, but still nothing. A week passed; every which way one looked on Wood Hill, the ground was covered with millions of tiny, frantic footprints. All the anthills had been trampled, each and every sagebrush squashed; rocks and dirt were flung far and wide across the cratered landscape. Still, no samurai sword!

How Terry ever explained the samurai sword's disappearance to his father I don't know. And I suppose I never will because not long afterward, Terry's family moved away, and for the next several years the tiny two-room house where they'd lived was home to a solitary bachelor of Japanese descent. In some peculiar way, I always felt there must be a cosmic connection between Mr. Mota and Hirohito's lost sword. For years afterward I never went hiking but what I stopped to investigate every promising cairn, but the only treasure I ever uncovered was a rusty Prince Albert tobacco tin, with a piece of paper inside, signifying a prospector's claim.

When I wasn't out in the foothills searching for buried treasure, I'd hang out at home, following my mother from room to room as she went about her housecleaning chores. My older brothers were in school, and besides me, the only other human beings Mom encountered during the day were the postman, the milkman, the Culligan man, the Fuller Brush man, and Mr. Emory—the dry cleaning man. Of these, Mr. Emory was my favorite because he always carried in his pants pocket a jumbo pack of Juicy Fruit chewing gum, which he dispensed like genius grants from the John D. and Catherine T. MacArthur Foundation to little kids along his route. I say genius grants because only those children who didn't ask for a stick of gum got one. Stand there and look stupid and he'd hand you a stick—but if you opened your mouth or even so much as held your hand out, he'd brush past as if you were invisible. Thus, even as behavioral scientist B.F. Skinner was turning pigeons into pecking machines, Mr. Emory was transforming the children in Carbondale into gum-cracking mutes. "Ask not and ye shall receive;" that's what I learned from Mr. Emory the dry cleaning man.

Besides deliverymen and door-to-door salesmen, our only link to the outside world was the radio. Mom kept the Stromberg-Carlson on all the time, and thus I became familiar with such names as Arthur Godfrey, Don McNeal, Jack Bailey, Lowell Thomas, and J. Edgar Hoover. The voice I remember best belonged to newscaster Gabriel Heatter. Heatter, like Godfrey, voiced his own commercial breaks, and no headline from the newscast could measure up to Heatter's melodious declaration: "WHEN I SAY COFFEE, I MEAN *FOLLLLGERS* COFFEE!"

Because I was not yet as tall as a Stromberg-Carlson radio, I had the impression Heatter's thundering testimonials originated from somewhere high in the sky. That impression was bolstered by the fact that Gabriel was also the name of an angel. Thus, whenever I heard him speak of coffee, I pictured the clouds parting as a radiant beam of sunlight burst upon the startled denizens of an Edward Hopperesque diner. Like deer caught in the headlights, they freeze in midsip, all faces turning heavenward as their white ceramic mugs clatter to the floor.

"*INFIDELS, REPENT*! WHEN I SAID COFFEE, I DIDN'T MEAN HILLS BROTHERS OR MJB. I MEANT *FOLLLGER'S* COFFEE! THOU SHALT HAVE NO OTHER BRANDS BEFORE MINE!"

Perhaps Heatter is the reason my parents both drank coffee—despite belonging to a church that preaches against the beverage almost as enthusiastically as Gabriel Heatter spoke in favor of it. To be sure, they never partook in public or at social functions that involved fellow Mormons. To do so would have set tongues awag throughout the ward. *What would other people think?* At first I was confused; however, in time I came to understand that, if you're a Mormon, nothing matters more than what the neighbors might think.

CHAPTER TWO

JESUS WANTS ME FOR A SOMETHING

There are people for whom religion is a full-time preoccupation. However, in our family, religion was something we tried not to think about except on Sundays. And even on Sundays I spent precious little time thinking about whatever it is people are supposed to think about when in church. Mainly, I just enjoyed being there. I enjoyed being part of the group. I enjoyed the camaraderie, and the warm pious feeling I got from sitting through Junior Sunday School services dressed in uncomfortable clothing. I enjoyed being a good little boy.

Most of all I enjoyed the music. My favorite Junior Sunday School song was "Jesus Wants Me for a Sunbeam." I especially enjoyed the chorus, a lilting refrain that inevitably set the juvenile choir swaying to and fro:

A sun-beam, a sun-beam,

Jesus wants me for a sunnn-beam;

A sun-beam, a sun-beam,

I'll be a sun-beam for Him.

Thanks to bad acoustics and the fact I couldn't yet read, for a long time I labored under the impression that what Jesus wanted me to become was "a something." Meantime, the kid seated next to me was eagerly anticipating the day he would turn into a "Jim Beam."

Another songbook favorite was "Give, Said the Little Stream"—a paean to irrigation—and "The Itsy Bitsy Spider"—a motivational ditty celebrating a persistent arachnid's determination to ascend a waterspout. What we enjoyed most about the song was the accompanying stage business: one hand playing the part of the spider, the opposite forearm (or the nearest girl's neck!) serving as waterspout.

At the conclusion of the opening song, we'd be treated to an inspirational story from the *Book of Mormon*. Whereas the tenets of other faiths are inscribed on scrolls or stone tablets, the basics of Mormonism are portrayed on something called a *flannel board*. Each Sunday our teacher would set up the board and then commence attaching various cutout figures of bearded middle-aged white men attired in sandals and bathrobes. Members of a vanished civilization known as the Nephites, essentially what they did was stand upon craggy hilltops under tumultuous skies, gazing sternly in the direction of a distant plain, where a great and bloody battle raged. Once the fight had ended, they'd record the event in "Reformed Egyptian" shorthand, on plates of solid gold.

Another gospel lesson featured a flannel facsimile of the church's founder, Joseph Smith, kneeling in a grove of trees, illuminated by a brilliant shaft of sunlight. In that shaft of sunlight hovers a translucent figure in a bright white bathrobe. It is the angel Moroni come to tell Smith where to dig in order to uncover those gilded records of pre-Columbian mayhem.

The account of how Joseph Smith, a poor uneducated farm boy from upstate New York, who conversed with angels and dug for buried treasure, definitely struck a responsive chord in me. Wasn't I also poor and uneducated? And had I not spent an inordinate amount of time combing the hills in search of buried treasure? And lo, verily, hadn't I likewise spent much time on my knees praying, in hopes an angel might appear to show me exactly where to dig?

Most of all, I could relate to the part about how young Joseph Smith had searched high and low for "the one and only true church." As a boy he'd investigated all of the major religions in his New York neighborhood—Presbyterian, Methodist, and Baptist—yet had come away unsatisfied. Finally he'd prayed for guidance, whereupon a heavenly messenger informed him that none of the churches in upstate New York was the true one. They were, in fact, an "abomination" in God's sight. "They draw near to me with their lips, but their hearts are far from me...."

What appealed to me was the *certitude* of the revelation. No gray areas, no qualifiers, no beating about the burning bush. How many times had I fervently wished such a messenger had appeared back when Terry and I were bickering over who was the one true king of the cowboys, or which of the four or five singers we'd heard of was the world's best? How I had *wished* I could snap my fingers, whereupon the heavens would part, and a big booming voice like that of Gabriel Heatter's would inform Terry in no uncertain terms that Frank Sinatra was definitely *not* so hotra, but just a punk kid from New Jersey with ties to organized crime.

"He draws near to the microphone with his lips, but never will he hit a high C the way Mario Lanza, and *only* Mario Lanza can."

Put another way, what Smith's fellow New Englander Ralph Waldo Emerson might have dismissed as a foolish consistency, we little-minded hobgoblins of Carbondale, Utah, hailed as wonderful news. Thanks to Joseph Smith, we knew for a certainty that ours was the only true church, and so we need not investigate any others. Also, now that we had the *Book of Mormon*, we could pretty much ignore all the other books in the public library. Who needs a whole library when the one book you have on your shelf is "the most correct" of them all?

The service concluded with a self-congratulatory hymn, "I Am a Child of God," after which a closing prayer was offered up by a volunteer from the congregation. And by closing prayer, I mean extemporaneous talk. Although each begins with the same salutation ("Our Heavenly Father ...") and concludes with the obligatory ending ("... in the name of Jesus Christ, Amen."), everything in between is ad lib. This is especially true whenever a grown-up steps to the podium, closes his eyes and opens his mouth. If there happens to be a political crisis brewing, it's a good bet he'll ask God to watch over the President and make sure he doesn't forget that we are a God-fearing nation. And of course, one always asks Heavenly Father to safeguard the health of the church president and to watch over those serving in the mission field.

In addition, it's always a good idea to acknowledge the Holy Ghost, whose abiding presence everyone in attendance has surely felt.

Ideally, one should affect a sonorous, oleaginous delivery peculiar to Mormon speakers. Once one settles into *that* groove, there's no limit to how long a prayer might drag on. If not for fidgeting toddlers and numerous infants bawling to have their diapers changed, I'm confident Mormon prayers would never end, but would go on and on forever.

I never liked it when Sunday school meetings ran late because it cut into the few precious hours of freedom I had before it was time to suit up for sacrament meeting. Sacrament meeting took place at six in the evening except on the first Sunday of each month, when it followed immediately on the heels of Sunday school. "Fast and Testimonial Meeting" it was called then, or "fast meeting" for short.

Fast meetings are anything but fast and short, and even less structured than opening and closing prayers. Essentially it's an open-mike forum, during which members of the congregation are encouraged to stand before the group and, as in the days of Moroni, "speak ... concerning the welfare of their souls."

Contemporary Mormons call it "bearing one's testimony," and it's something you're expected to do at regular intervals if you wish to be considered a saint in good standing.

Typically, Bishop Smart would kick things off by bearing his testimony from the pulpit. Like all Mormon clergy, Bishop Smart was an unpaid layman.

He'd spent no time in divinity school, although as a young man he'd undergone two years of total immersion in missionary work. He'd returned from the mission field convinced that the Gospel as revealed to Joseph Smith is *true*. Such was the mantra he'd shared with many a gentile on his mission; such was the mantra he'd repeated time and again since his return. And as always, he concluded with the line: "... and I say these things in the name of Jesus Christ, amen."

At this point the bishop would take his seat and a lengthy silence would ensue as members of the congregation waited to be prompted by the Holy Ghost. Almost always the Spirit's first nudge was felt by Sister Lucille Bensen, the ward's unofficial ice breaker.

"Well, I would just like to say that I, too, feel in my heart that the Gospel is true," she would begin. "I know that Heavenly Father cares about each and every one of us, and I'd like to add I'm especially thankful today for all the wonderful blessings He has bestowed upon our family. I'm thankful for my lovely daughter GarLene, who has just won a spot on the Carbondale High School cheerleading squad, and who has also made the honor roll. And for my dear husband, recently appointed assistant superintendent at the Horse Canyon Mine. And I say these things in the name of Jesus Christ, amen."

Having thrown down the gauntlet, Sister Bensen would sit. Then Sister Johnson would rise. "My dear brothers and sisters, I would like to take this opportunity to stand before you today and bear my testimony that the Gospel of the Church of Jesus Christ of Latter-day Saints is true, and to thank Heavenly

Father for all the many wonderful blessings He has bestowed upon *our* family. As many of you may have already heard, my husband was recently promoted to general manager at the Wellington coal washing plant, and we have recently moved into a lovely new home. And I would also like to express my gratitude for my six wonderful children, four of whom are on the honor roll—including Eldon, who recently turned nineteen and is looking forward to his mission call. And I say these things in the name of Jesus Christ, amen."

Things were really rolling now; everyone in the congregation who had a job or a kid was beginning to feel the presence of the Holy Ghost. Sister Snow stood to announce that *all* of her remaining five sons were determined to follow in the footsteps of Spencer, currently serving in the Eastern Albanian mission field. She shared an excerpt from a letter Eldon had sent home, boasting of "fantastic" experiences he'd had among the Eastern Albanians and of how much his own testimony of the truthfulness of the gospel had grown since he left Carbondale.

"After Spencer returns from his mission," Sister Snow concluded evenly, "he plans to get married in the temple and attend Brigham Young University. And I say these things in the name of Jesus Christ, amen."

Upon hearing of Spencer's plans, a young woman by the name of Sharlene squirmed in a front pew. At the time Spencer had been called to serve his mission, Sharlene had been his steady squeeze. But that was eleven long months ago, and now it was common knowledge to everyone in the ward except Sister Snow (and Elder Spencer!) that Sharlene had found herself a new boyfriend. Of course, this didn't necessarily mean that Spencer couldn't still get married in the temple when he got back to Utah. It only meant that the wet dreams he was currently experiencing in Eastern Albania were even more "fantastic" than even he imagined.

Throughout the meeting, the Holy Ghost's influence would ebb and flow, and from time to time it would drift away entirely. Whenever it did, a minute, maybe two, would pass without anyone rising to address the congregation. The longer the silence, the more the tension would build. Presently, young girls seated in the front pews would commence giggling and elbowing one another, until at last one of them would be goaded into action. A prepubescent blond would abruptly stand and deliver a brief, incoherent testimonial: "I'm thankful for ... mumble, mumble ... in the name of Jesus Christ, amen." Then she'd drop back into her seat, slapping a hand over her mouth to suppress a giggle. Immediately the blond head next to her would pop up; there'd be another incoherent declaration of faith, followed by the obligatory giggle.

On and on it would go, little heads popping up and down in rapid succession like the carnival game Whack-A-Mole. Once begun, it wouldn't stop unless an older person intervened—either Bishop Smart or one of his two counselors. Or better still, the man I will call *Jebediah Bangerter*.

I call him that because it wasn't his real name, and I wish to spare his descendants and friends the embarrassment that might result from an accurate description of the man. Quite often in this memoir, I have changed names to spare both the guilty and the innocent, partly for merciful reasons and partly because I couldn't decide which were which.

Brother Bangerter was by far the oldest member of our ward, a sequoia among saplings. Legend had it he'd been born in a covered wagon and came of age in the day when polygamist church leaders were more likely to wear prison stripes than pin stripes. He'd served a difficult mission in the Midwest, where he'd been sniped at by Lutherans and had taken a Comanche arrow in the shoulder. Such hardships and persecutions had only served to strengthen his conviction that the restored gospel was true, albeit much changed over the many decades since he'd been baptized. For example, Mormonism in Bangerter's youth was a lot more magical. It wasn't at all unusual for saints to be visited by heavenly messengers during the week as they toiled in their fields—angels such as the one that had appeared to John Koyle of Salem, Utah—and showed the farmer where he should dig in order to find a treasure trove of Nephite gold.

Brother Bangerter himself was heavily invested in stock of the mining company founded upon Koyle's vision, which to date has failed to discover the treasure. Moreover, he was the only saint in our ward who had ever spoken "in tongues." Supposedly the same language Adam spoke, today it sounds like gibberish to all except listeners likewise possessed of the Holy Ghost.

At the time he was ordained an "elder" at the tender age of nineteen, a church patriarch had placed his hands on Brother Bangerter's head and promised that if he were to follow the Lord's commandments and obey the Word of Wisdom, he would live to see the Second Coming.

Since that day, Jebediah Bangerter had celebrated almost eighty birthdays, and from the looks of him, the Second Coming was just around the corner. Indeed, the world might very well come to an end even before this particular fast and testimony meeting would. In which case, the prudent thing would have been for me to leap to my feet immediately and pledge my everlasting faith and allegiance to Joseph Smith and the restored gospel of Jesus Christ. But for some reason I never did.

Part of the problem, no doubt, lay in the fact I was a shy child by nature. The other part: Never once had I sensed the presence of the Holy Ghost. Many were the Sundays I'd shut my eyes, concentrate, and do my very best to let the spirit in—but still, *nothing*. Perhaps sitting bolt upright on a hard wooden pew isn't the ideal position for receiving revelation, I thought. Perhaps I should drop to my knees. Or better still, wander off into the woods and drop to my knees there.

I was more than relieved when finally Bishop Smart's soothing voice broke through the awful quiet that was welling up inside of me.

"I'd like to thank those who have shared their testimonies with us on this fine Sabbath," he announcd. "I am convinced the spirit of the Holy Ghost has been with us today. I'm sure each and every one of us has felt His presence."

The service concluded with a song from the hymnal, led by ward chorister Helene Bromwell. Unlike the rest of us, Sister Bromwell was endowed with a lovely singing voice and perfect pitch. To lead a congregation that couldn't carry a tune entailed some heavy lifting on her part, but somehow she managed to shepherd us through all four verses of "Come, Come Ye Saints." At long last came the closing prayer, and provided we were lucky and the Holy Ghost didn't intervene, six long hours after it had begun, so-called Fast Sunday would finally draw to an end.

    I'd follow my nose home, to the kitchen where Mom was busy preparing the regulation Sunday dinner of pot roast, mashed potatoes, green peas, fresh baked bread, and homemade pie for dessert. Having skipped breakfast, we tucked in like famine victims. Once my plate was cleaned, I was free to change into my regular uniform of blue jeans and T-shirt and settle myself on the carpet in front of the Stromberg Carlson for an afternoon of audio entertainment. Radio legends such as Jack Benny and Fred Allen, Fibber McGee and Molly, Amos 'n' Andy, were still on the air, as were adventure serials such as The Green Hornet and Flash Gordon. My favorite program was "The Shadow," a drama featuring crime fighter LaMont Cranston, who, in the course of his travels through the Orient had acquired the power to "cloud men's minds." Bad guys couldn't see Cranston, but they could *feel* his presence in the room. Exactly as everybody in the ward fully anticipated I would one day be able to sense the presence of the Holy Ghost—if only I could banish those pesky clouds from my mind.

CHAPTER THREE

NOT-SO-FAST TIMES AT WARREN G. HARDING ELEMENTARY

Since neither of my parents had ever cracked the *Book of Mormon* or stood up in a testimony meeting, I had a hard time gauging the depth of their religious convictions. One thing they did believe was that the church was a nice institution, with the power to keep kids from going astray. They felt confident that regular church attendance would turn me into a good citizen, same as sending me to public school would result in my becoming educated. It was the way people in America thought back then and the way most Americans still think today. Institutions are the way to go.

Between my parents and my teachers, there was never any interaction whatever; in fact, Mom didn't even bother to take me to school on my first day. She just pointed me in the direction of Warren G. Harding Elementary and said, "*Go!*"

Warren G. Harding gave me my first glimpse into the secular world that lay beyond the ward boundaries, and what variegated world it proved to be! There were Mexican kids from the south side of town, Greek and Italian kids who'd been bused in from outlying mining camps. There were hillbillies of unknown ethnic origin who'd roamed wild as coyotes on so-called "ranches" that were without running water or indoor plumbing. Many appeared to be taking their very first steps in store-bought shoes.

There were an astonishing number of little girls named either Susan or Linda—the apparent result of names having been rationed during the war years.

Needless to say, I was terrified. However, my fears eased somewhat after I learned I'd been assigned to Miss Burton, a spinster schoolmarm reputed to be the sweetest, kindest, most tolerant adult in town. Unfortunately, no sooner had I taken my seat than Principal Madsen popped in to announce I'd been transferred to Mrs. Algiers's class. Mrs. Algiers's standing on the sweetness scale was several notches below that of Miss Burton; nonetheless, I took some consolation in knowing I was far better off than those unfortunate souls who'd been assigned to Mrs. Spigott.

No sooner had I gotten settled than Principal Madsen reappeared. Next thing I knew, I was a ward of Mrs. Spigott!

The three tiers of public education I experienced that day mirrored what I'd been taught in Sunday school about the three levels of celestial glory. Being transferred from Miss Burton's to Mrs. Algier's class, had I not immediately sensed a major difference—"as that of the moon differs from the sun in the firmament?"

Then finally came Mrs. Spigott—neither the moon nor the sun, but rather the crab nebula.

Our desks were straight out of the nineteenth century, ornamented on the sides with cast iron scrollwork, encrusted underneath with barnacle-like wads of chewing gum. Numerous initials and signatures had been carved into my desk top, names of prominent citizens of Carbondale, including that of Bishop Smart. It was hard for me to picture Bishop Smart as a boy—or, for that matter, myself as an adult. It was all very confusing.

At midmorning, noon, and again in the afternoon we were turned loose for recess. The Lindas and Susans assembled at one end of the playground to play hopscotch and skip rope, while the boys engaged in rougher games such as crack-the-whip and king-of-the-hill.

Every day I witnessed numerous shoving matches and fist fights, the result of ongoing, unresolved conflicts. Who is king of the cowboys? The world's greatest singer? I had my opinions, but I stayed out of it. Last thing I needed was another scar.

My instincts told me the best way to survive Warren G. Harding was to remain as inconspicuous as possible, and before long I became as invisible as LaMont Cranston. Even when I thought I knew the answer to one of Mrs. Spigott's questions, I resisted the temptation to raise my hand. I strove hard not to excel at playground games, nor did I take sides in playground debates. However, I had one talent that, try as I might, I couldn't hide beneath a bushel. Without even trying, I became the greatest speller in the history of Warren G. Harding Elementary.

Where the gift came from I can't say; I only know that once I saw a word in print, from that moment on I could spell it. By the time I entered second grade, all I had to do was *hear* the word spoken. I never needed to sound out the syllables; I merely repeated the letters as they appeared, always in proper order, on the blackboard of my mind.

Miss Wilson was my teacher now, and once a week she'd subject the class to a spelling bee. Everyone would line up along one wall, and then Miss Wilson would open her dictionary and commence firing. If you misspelled a word, you had to sit down. If at the end you were the last kid standing, Miss Wilson would hand you a nickel for ice cream and let you go home early. That last kid standing, first to go home, was always me.

Free at last, I'd linger awhile on the pavement below Miss Wilson's classroom in hopes of being noticed by Judy, a pretty classmate whose heart I imagined would one day be captured by the only second grader in town who could spell "refrigerator." It didn't matter to me that Judy couldn't spell C-A-T; I'd fallen madly in love with her, if for no other reason than because I needed someone to play the part of the damsel in distress in my romantic daydreams.

The long solitary trek home afforded ample opportunity to flesh out the plot. Storylines varied; one day it might be rampaging Indians who'd tied Judy to a tree, the next day she'd be in the clutches of a band of pirates. The main thing was that Judy had to be in distress—and only I, Captain Spellright, could save her. Each episode in the ongoing saga featured the same rapturous ending—yet in real life the gulf separating us never narrowed a whit.

Part of the problem lay in the fact the two sexes were in those days segregated from birth. The girls occupied one side of the playground, the boys the other. No way could I stroll over to where Judy and her friends were playing. No way could I ever join in a game of jump rope or jacks, and certainly there was no way in hell I'd ever screw up the courage to open my mouth and talk to her. No, my only hope was that a gang of international terrorists would take Judy hostage, and refuse to turn her loose until someone came along who could correctly spell the word "refrigerator."

About the only time Judy wasn't being held captive in my daydreams was Wednesday afternoons, when instead of ambling homeward after school I walked directly to the ward house to attend Primary. A sort of after-school extended care program for Mormon children under the age of twelve, Primary was far and away my favorite church meeting. For one thing, it was permissible to attend in jeans and a T-shirt. For another, there was no preaching, no testimony bearing, no windy passages from the *Book of Mormon* to memorize. Mainly, it was fun and games, a wild romp on the well-worn hardwood floors of the ward recreation hall.

In other words, Primary was church without the churchiness, and I enjoyed it so much that over the course of four years I never missed a single meeting—a feat that earned me a four-year perfect attendance pin minted by the O.C. Tanner Jewelry Company in Salt Lake City.

Other prizes could be won at Primary—good conduct medals and service badges. These were displayed on a green felt sash worn over one shoulder like a baldric, which we called a "bandelo." Bedecked in medals, badges and pins, Primary was a place that closely resembled the rich fantasy world I'd constructed in my head, a world in which I was a hero, a leader of men and savior of young women.

After Primary let out, the boys would gather on the chapel lawn for a rousing game of "Pomp." The last player to declare himself "not it" would be stationed in the middle of the field; the "not its" formed a phalanx along one side. Then the player in the middle would cry "Pomp!"—whereupon the not-its would charge like a herd of thirst-crazed wildebeests.

If you made it to the far side of the playing field without being caught, you remained free. If not, you joined the ranks of the captured, and became one of the pursuers in the next round. As the game progressed, there'd be an ever-expanding ratio of pursuers to pursue, more and more catchers in the middle and an ever-diminishing number of free-range Mormons.

Though I was not particularly swift, I was usually one of the last runners caught. Like LaMont Cranston, I had acquired an uncanny ability to cloud my playmates' minds, so that it was not until late in the game that I would finally be noticed. Once that happened, of course, the odds against my remaining free rose sharply.

Many years later I would find myself playing a similar game against twenty thousand Mormons massed upon the grassy campus of Brigham Young University. The odds against me then would be infinitely greater than anything I had ever experienced as a seven-year-old—a time in my life when being a member in good standing of the majority appealed to me much more than being a maverick. Which is why I was eagerly looking forward to April 6, the day I would turn eight years of age—old enough at last to be formally inducted into the Church of Jesus Christ of Latter-day Saints.

CHAPTER FOUR

GOING DOWN FOR THE COUNT

Time and again in Junior Sunday School the point had been made that eight is the proper age for children to be baptized. Of equal importance, that it be baptism "by total immersion." The act of sprinkling water on a newborn infant's head—in our minds—was an act of child abuse.

Anything that smacked of Catholicism, in fact, was wrong. Consider, for example, the precept that babies come into the world tainted by original sin. The Prophet Joseph Smith strenuously objected to the notion, declaring that "men will be punished for their own sins, and not for Adam's transgression."

That struck me as fair. I was in hot water enough, having recently been caught helping myself to Old Lady Fox's apricots—so why should I also be held accountable for forbidden fruit plucked six thousand years before I was born?

What appealed to me most about Mormon baptism was that all of the black marks accumulated over the course of my first eight years would be stricken from the record. I would emerge from the baptismal font pure as the fresh-fallen snow. If I were to slip on the wet tile floor and brain myself, I'd go straight to the Celestial Kingdom. There'd be no inqui-sition regarding purloined apricots, no nettle-some questions regarding what had possessed me to build a bonfire in the basement, no taped replay of the time I'd uttered a bad word within earshot of my mother.

What I wasn't looking forward to was total immer-sion. Thanks to what I'd been told as a child, I was deathly afraid of canals, rivers, irrigation ditches, swimming pools and baptismal fonts. And regardless of what I'd been taught in Junior Sunday School, I thought sprinkling might be the better way to go.

"There's nothing to be afraid of, silly," Mom as-sured me. "Just shut your eyes and close your mouth and you'll be just fine." My older brother Chuck was less helpful, and taunted me for days on end. "Crybaby, tittie mouse, laid an egg in our house...."

"Tittie mouse." It so happened that "tit" was the bad word I'd been punished for saying. Mom had punished me by putting hot pepper on my tongue, which might have worked if *only* I had been able to make a connection between the crime and the pun-ishment. Indeed, if *only* I had been aware of having committed a crime! After all, it was just a word I'd heard at school—same as "teat." Miss Wilson had used the latter word to describe that part of a cow from which comes milk, whereupon the entire class had broken into laughter.

"What's so funny?" she asked.

"It's not 'teat,'" explained a small voice from the back row. It's 'tit.'"

As the snows of winter subsided and my birthday grew nigh, my fears continued to mount. The person who would be performing the baptism was 21-year-old Elder Gillman, recently returned from the mission field. I didn't know Gillman well; in fact, the two of us had yet to meet. And, of course, he would know nothing about my hydrophobia. Was there a chance he might launch into one of those lengthy extemporaneous Mormon prayers while he held me under, I wondered? My God—I'll be a floater before he gets halfway to "amen."

April arrived—less than a week to go before my eighth birthday. Any serious sinning I intended to indulge in before the slate would be wiped clean. I had better get started. Unfortunately, the range of temptations available to a seven-year-old is somewhat narrow. Was I to covet my neighbor's wife? Bow down to graven images? Of the Ten Commandments, so far I'd broken only two: the eighth (stealing Old Lady Fox's apricots) and the ninth (giving her a fictitious name when caught). So I'd be going into the baptismal font relatively sin free, like unworn underwear going into the Twin Tub Dexter.

I was in fact wearing brand-new underwear—also a white shirt, white pants, white socks—white *everything*. Even my face was white; the prospect of being totally immersed scared me stiff.

Next thing I knew, the two of us were standing knee-deep in warmish water. Feeling Elder Gillman's hand on my shoulder, I drew a deep breath and squeezed my eyelids shut. I kept them shut as he intoned gravely: "In the name of the Father, the Son, and the Holy Ghost, and through the power of the priesthood vested in me—"

Then suddenly Elder Gillman clapped his other hand over my mouth, using his thumb and forefinger to pinch my nostrils shut. *Kersplash*! Down I went. *Gasp*! Up I came.

A murmur swept across the gallery, a sign that something was amiss. "His right foot didn't go under," I heard someone say.

Again, Elder Gillman lay a firm hand on my shoulder. He began anew: "In the name of the Father, the Son and the Holy Ghost, and through the power vested—"

I drew another deep breath, shut my eyes. Elder Gillman covered my mouth. Down I went. Up I came. *Gasp*. More murmuring from the gallery.

"His foot *still* didn't go under," I heard someone say. "His foot was mostly under, but his big toe was sticking up."

Elder Gillman breathed a heavy sigh. His hand wasn't just resting on my shoulder now; he was holding me in a manner similar to how a bald eagle clasps a salmon.

"In the name of the Father, the Son, and the Holy Ghost—" he repeated evenly.

"*Ow!*"

My cry was cut short when Elder Gillman clamped his other hand over my mouth.

"... and through the power of the priesthood vested in me ..."

"Mmmfph."

This time Elder Gillman didn't merely lay me down, but roughly *shoved* me under. And somehow managed to keep me down, no matter that I was thrashing like an alligator. By the time it was over, Elder Gillman was soaked from head to toe—ditto the witnesses. As for me, I'd finally gone completely under, and come up a Latter-day Saint. I was now a member in good standing of the one and only true church on the face of the earth. Best of all, I was without sin, and remained that way for most of the afternoon.

CHAPTER FIVE

ALL WORK AND NO PAY AT THE DESERET NEWS

Put your shoulder to the wheel, push a-law-ong;

Do your duty with a heart full of saw-ong.

We all have work, let no one shirk;

Put your shoul-der to the whee-eel.

It was one of my favorite hymns, what with its lilting melody and lyrics rich in swooping diphthongs and superfluous syllables. Plus, it was a song about hard labor—a subject about which I was no stranger. My first job opportunity had come early, as I was walking down a dark hallway at Warren G. Harding, when suddenly out of the inky shadows emerged the school's custodian, old Mr. Morley.

"Young man," he announced, "I've just finished reviewing your application, and I've decided you're just the person I've been looking for to fill the post of assistant janitor. How soon can you start?"

"*Assistant janitor?*" said my mother at the supper table that evening. "That sounds like a pretty good deal. But I think you're too young to take on that much responsibility. You should let Chuck take it."

That's the way things always went in our family; I never got anything until after my older brother had either outgrown it or worn it out. In turn, everything that Chuck ever owned was a hand-me-down from Jim—including the beat-up Schwinn bicycle, astride which he managed the family paper route. The route number—how can I ever forget it?—was 206-C. The paper route, too, was a hand-me-down.

"Chuck can take the assistant janitor job," my mother continued, "and you can take over the paper route."

For once, I wasn't terribly disappointed. Compared to pushing a broom and scrubbing toilets, delivering newspapers didn't look all that bad. It was healthy, outdoor exercise with a shallow learning curve. Matter of fact, I already knew the route by heart, having substituted for Chuck on numerous occasions.

At three o'clock the following afternoon Chuck ceremoniously turned over the newspaper bag and the Schwinn. Come suppertime, he asked for his stuff back. Evidently the position of assistant janitor of Warren G. Harding Elementary School wasn't as good as it sounded.

If old Mr. Morley ever caught on that it was a different kid that reported for work the following afternoon, he never let on. He just handed me the dust mop and ordered me to get moving. "Start at the top floor," he said, "and work your way down."

I didn't need a map to find my way around, for by this time I'd been incarcerated at Warren G. Harding for five years and was well-acquainted with her dimly-lit, oregano-scented corridors. The only rooms that were new to me were the janitor's closet, the boiler room and, of course, the girl's washroom.

Last stop in my rounds was the ground floor classroom of Miss Kate Swift, who'd been my fourth grade teacher and who, as far as I could tell, was the only person in Carbondale who believed there was the remotest chance in hell I'd ever amount to anything.

"Well, hello, Richard," she chirped as I jockeyed my broom past her desk. "How have you been?"

"I'm the new assistant janitor," I said. I held out my broom and dustpan as if to say, "Look on my works, ye mighty, and despair!"

Miss Swift shook her head. She was a well-educated woman, pretty, and bore no resemblance to the crabby Mrs. Spigott. A native of Ohio, she'd ventured West in hopes of rescuing the culturally deprived children of rural Utah from the grip of ignorance and superstition. Many small towns across America have at least one such idealistic educator, just as every small town has its drunk. All too often, alas, it's the same person.

Once I was done sweeping and dusting Warren G. Harding Elementary from top to bottom, I'd descend the long, narrow stairwell that led to Mr. Morley's "office" in the basement boiler room. There he lay, stretched out on a dirty mattress on the floor, dead to the world.

I'd stow my push broom in the broom closet—as old Morley had taught me—handle down so the bristles wouldn't get permanently bent. It's probably the one and only thing I ever learned at Harding Elementary that I haven't since forgotten. Oh, wait! I also remember that the job of assistant janitor paid two dollars and fifty cents—per *week*! Payday was on Friday; I'd shake old Morley awake and he'd fish two silver dollars and a four-bit piece from his pants pocket. It was never paper money and never a check; in fact, there was no paperwork whatever involved in Morley's janitorial operation. More than once I wondered how my boss managed to keep track of things, what with no desk, no ledgers, no filing cabinet, and no personnel files.

Come to think on it, I have no recollection of ever having applied for the position of assistant janitor!

I stayed on for only a few weeks, until my brother Chuck succeeded in finding a job at a gas station, whereupon I took over operation of route 206-C. No one ever bothered to notify the circulation department at Deseret News headquarters in Salt Lake City of the change. What business was it of theirs, so long as the newspapers got delivered?

Route 206-C had been in our family for six years. Jim had run it first, in typical Horatio Alger fashion. During his three-year tenure, the number of subscribers had risen to over a hundred—all of them satisfied customers. The newspaper always came on time; never torn or wet. Never once had a tossed newspaper punched a hole through a screen door, landed on a rooftop, or been swallowed by a pyracantha bush.

In fact, never in the entire history of the Deseret News has there ever been a carrier as determined and conscientious as my brother Jim. The time he was struck by a car, he asked the ambulance driver if he'd mind making a few stops along Carbon Avenue on the way to the hospital.

Middle brother Chuck's management style differed somewhat, so that by the time I inherited the route, subscribers numbered fewer than fifty. Rare was the screen door that still included a screen; rarer still, a rooftop unadorned by at least one yellowing issue of the Deseret News. Motorists who previously had swerved to avoid running over the paperboy now swerved toward him.

It didn't help that delivering the Deseret News was a money-losing proposition, thanks to a system whereby carriers consistently absorbed the bulk of the publication's operating costs. It worked like this: Each carrier received a monthly bill for however many newspapers he'd been shipped; it was the carrier's responsibility to collect from his customers, and anything left over after he paid his monthly bill was his theoretical profit.

In the unlikely event everyone along my route were to pay up, I'd pocket twenty dollars for the month. However, if only ten customers refused to answer when I rang the doorbell—or skipped town or pled poverty—then my income dropped to zero. And on Route 206-C, a monthly average of ten deadbeats was a certainty.

When I ran these figures past my mother, she responded the way she always did whenever I complained about my lot in life.

"Your father and I had to work when we were your age," she said. "Our parents didn't give us everything we wanted."

"I'm not asking you for anything," I whined. "I'm only saying that the problem with working for the Deseret News is that it pays nothing."

But the look on her face told me it was no use complaining. No matter how bad things got for me, they'd never compare with the way things were during the Great Depression. My parents' suffering, in turn, was nothing compared to the short, brutish existence of my grandparents. "Thank your lucky stars for the smallpox vaccination." "Praise God there are no grizzly bears along your route!"

The only sympathetic ears around were those attached to the heads of my fellow paperboys, all of whom agreed that peddling the Deseret News was barely a step above slavery. In fact, the better portion of each working day was passed grousing about our mean working conditions, at a location known as the "paper stop."

The paper stop was a vacant lot in the middle of town landscaped with Russian thistles and furnished with an incinerator. Around three o'clock every weekday afternoon a Wycoff delivery van would arrive and drop off several bundles of newspapers. Then it would pull away, almost always trailing a tin can or a dead cat, affixed to the tailgate by a generous length of baling wire. If it was wintertime, the first order of the day was to start a fire in the incinerator. Fuel consisted of bundle wrappers and advertising supplements. On really chilly days, entire sections might go up in smoke; it all depended upon how cold it was and whether any sections of the newspaper were worth saving, in our opinion.

Something we never torched, however, was the Saturday insert known as the Church News, which was more eagerly anticipated by Desert News subscribers than the Sunday funnies, no matter that each new issue was pretty much the same as the one before. On the inside front page was a weekly uplifting message from the president and reigning prophet of the Mormon Church, David O. McKay. On the back page was an editorial penned by the church's resident curmudgeon, Mark E. Peterson. Anyone who didn't believe the world was fast going to hell in a hand basket had only to read one of Peterson's weekly diatribes in order to be set straight.

Church News articles were written in a language similar to what I'd heard spoken in church on Sundays. Instead of Mr. this and Mrs. that, men and women were referred to as brothers and sisters. Sisters and Brothers were wont to get married, and as a general rule these unions would produce *no fewer than* six children. Custom dictated that at least one of those children be "currently enrolled" at Brigham Young University, and another "currently serving" in the mission field.

Meantime, the patriarch of the clan would be currently serving as president of whichever insurance, banking or investment company he happened to be affiliated with. His resume would also include a list of religious pursuits—beginning with the two-year mission he had served as a young man, before coming home and enrolling at Brigham Young, where almost immediately he had become engaged to Sister so-and-so, a homemaking major from Rupert, Idaho.

A brother bearing such impressive credentials was a prime candidate for induction into the ruling gerontocracy of the Mormon Church. But first, he and his wife would be called to administer one of the church's far-flung missions. As mission president, his job would be to coordinate and supervise the good work and to act as surrogate father to all the young men serving under him. His wife's job would be to act as surrogate mother.

The most amazing part: During their two-year tenure abroad, the couple would receive no salary whatsoever. They'd even pay their own expenses. This selfless spirit of service without compensation was the one thing righteous Mormon couples had in common with those of us who delivered the Deseret News.

I had a few subscribers along my route whose biographies vaguely resembled those profiled each week in the pages of the Church News—but their numbers were shrinking, thanks in no small part to the machinations of a fellow carrier by the name of Arnie Smart.

Arnie was the son of Bishop Smart, whose secular occupation was regional distribution agent for the Deseret News. As the boss's son, Arnie enjoyed certain occupational perks the rest of us could only dream about. On cold winter days when his Schwinn wouldn't start, he'd make the rounds in his mother's nice warm car. You'd never find him huddled with the unwashed masses at the paper stop; *au contraire,* it was Arnie who'd alerted his father to the fact advertising supplements were being used to stoke the incinerator. The following day, Bishop Smart had given the lot of us a stern lecture on the evils of burning newsprint. The day after that, Arnie's entire bundle became a yule log.

I won't say who struck the match; to do so would be to violate an oath of silence I swore in the presence of half a dozen witnesses—at least one of whom, I believe, was Sicilian. But yes, it *could* have been me. I certainly wasn't lacking for a motive; that's for sure—for not only was Arnie Smart a snitch, but he was forever trying to horn in on my territory.

It so happened that route 206-C covered what was arguably the most coveted real estate in town—the very center of Carbondale. It was a neighborhood of densely-packed dwellings with broad porches, few fences, and mostly friendly dogs. But every now and then as I was out delivering newspapers I'd come upon a sight that turned my stomach: Arnie Smart's bicycle!

Beginning back in the days when my brother Chuck ran the route, Arnie had been secretly proselytizing in 206-C territory, targeting those houses with battered storm doors and rooftops blanketed with newsprint. He enjoyed a particularly high rate of conversion among the elderly, seducing them with a promise to always place the newspaper under the mat. Is bending over a problem? He'll ring the doorbell. Eyesight failing? No problem—Arnie Smart will sit on your lap and *read* you the damn newspaper.

In the rapidly deteriorating vision of such folk, Arnie Smart was golden, the sort of lad destined to one day serve an honorable mission for the church, before returning to become a rising star in the life insurance industry, husband to some lucky gal from a small farming town in downstate Idaho, father to six children.

In the meantime, there'd be a few speed bumps along the path to perfection. For instance, there was the time he came tripping down the walk, having just serviced an elderly customer, only to discover his bicycle had gone missing. Three days later, police divers dredged it from the murky waters of the city irrigation canal, and although he was never formally charged with the crime, my brother Chuck was a person of interest. Even today, whenever a Schwinn is fished from the Carbondale irrigation canal, people say it was most likely "chucked" there.

To be fair, Arnie Smart wasn't the only reason my customer base was shrinking. It so happened that more than half the households along my route were non-Mormon and thus not at all enthusiastic about a newspaper that tended to read like a religious tract. They couldn't care less who was next in line to succeed David O. McKay as prophet, seer and revelator—or just how many subdivisions of glory awaited in the world to come. What they were mainly interested in was the day-to-day events of *this* world. Hence, they favored the Deseret News's rival, The Salt Lake Tribune.

Besides, the Tribune came in the morning—a time of day when coffee drinkers traditionally prefer to get their news fix. Even my own parents, inveterate coffee drinkers, were Tribune subscribers.

From time to time the Deseret News would attempt to remedy the situation by dispatching an agent we knew simply as "the solicitor." Bishop Smart would call to say the solicitor would be making the rounds of Carbondale that weekend; would I please meet him on Saturday morning at the Savoy Hotel?

The Savoy was an ancient edifice, a relic from the days when salesmen traveled from town to town by train. After a hard day of pounding the pavement, they'd catch a bite at the Grand Cafe across the street and perhaps attempt to score a date. Or else they'd just dial up Madam Trixie at The Star and ask to have a girl delivered. No doubt the Savoy had seen its share of stomping over the years; however, come Saturday morning as I tiptoed up the crepuscular stairwell, the resident mice were squeaking louder than the bedsprings.

I discovered the solicitor—I'll call him Willie—lying unconscious underneath a chenille bedspread, even deader to the world than the narcoleptic Mr. Morley. Getting him to his feet and dressed was no mean feat, and not until after he'd downed his third cup of coffee was he finally able to speak.

"Well, Mr. Mayonnaise, I suppose it's time we got down to business. Which way is your paper route?"

I steered Willie east to Carbon Avenue, then north two blocks to the southern boundary of 206-C country. The first dwelling we came to was a tidy white clapboard house with an aluminum screen door that looked as good as new. It was the residence of my former teacher Miss Kate Swift, obviously a non-subscriber.

I could tell by the look on her face when she came to the door that she was disappointed to discover her erstwhile promising pupil turned janitor, now in the company of an itinerant drunkard.

"Madam," Willie began, "I'd like you to meet Ricky Mendez. He's the official Desert News distribution agent in this neighborhood."

"*Desert* News?" Miss Swift furrowed her brow.

"Yes, Ma'am. It's a daily afternoon newspaper out of Salt Lake City that covers every aspect of the world and domestic scene that a woman like yourself could possibly be interested in. Plus, it's the only newspaper in the world in which you will find the Church News."

"Oh, the *Deseret* News. Yes, I've heard of it—"

"Only *good* things, I presume," Willie interjected hopefully.

"Well ..."

Again, Miss Swift furrowed her brow. She was, after all, a non-Mormon from out of state, unmarried, and resolutely uninterested in becoming a convert and eternal "helpmate" to some pompous patriarch, let alone bearing his equally pompous six children.

"I really don't think I'd be interested, Mr. ... uh ..."

"It's not for myself I'm asking, you understand," Willie countered, wedging a wing-tipped toe inside the screen door Miss Swift was attempting to shut. "It's for Ricky Mendez here. See, he's hoping to sign up enough new subscribers in order to win a free trip to Washington, D.C. ..."

"Oh?" Miss Swift and I responded in unison. It was the first mention I'd heard of a trip to Washington. Why on earth would the Deseret News want to send me to Washington?

"... to meet with his congressional representative and to visit the Lincoln Memorial and the Washington Monument," Willie continued without missing a beat. "And to have his picture taken with President Eisenhower in the Oval Office."

Wow! Total access! The longer Willie went on, the better it all sounded. Just how many new subscribers are we talking about, I wondered?

"How many new subscribers would he need to win the trip?" echoed Miss Swift.

"Well, he's *close*." Willie pursed his lips thoughtfully. "He's within, I would say, three or four...."

Miss Swift shifted her gaze to me. She knew now that Willie was lying through his teeth. What she couldn't figure was what had possessed me to change my name to Ricky Mendez—and what exactly was the nature of my relationship with this bottle-nosed buffoon?

Shutting the door in our faces, Kate Swift retreated to her study, making straight for the bottle of gin she kept hidden behind her bookcase. Whatever was I thinking when I moved to Utah? she wondered. *Why do I even try*?

All that morning and well into the afternoon, Willie and I continued to make the rounds. At each stop my name and job description were different, as was my alleged destination. One time it was New York City where top newsboys from around the country are feted; the next time it was San Francisco. Then it was San Diego, El Paso, Kansas City, Chicago, Cincinnati, Las Vegas, Albuquerque, and finally Tucumcari. I had to give Willie credit: The man had been around.

None too soon we arrived at the last house on the last street on the far edge of 206-C territory. To my relief no one was at home—at any rate, no one answered the doorbell. Willie shrugged, let loose an asthmatic sigh, and suggested we stop for a burger and a milk shake before calling it a day.

"I'd love to, Willie," I lied, "but I think I hear my mother calling."

"Aw, c'mon, Dickie. One milkshake ain't gonna hurt ya. It's my treat."

As ill luck would have it, we happened to be standing almost directly in front of a local eatery known as the Milky Way. So far I'd been lucky; what with the aliases and all, only Miss Swift had recognized me. But the Milky Way was a popular youth hangout, a place where my classmates liked to go for a coke and hamburger after the Saturday matinee let out. And here it was, Saturday afternoon.

Moreover, it was a Saturday afternoon in the middle of the 1950s, a pivotal time in American history. Young people were undergoing a paradigm shift—away from Mickey Rooney and toward James Dean. It was vitally important to look cool at all times—*especially* when fellow hepcats in the next banquette were checking you out. Above all, it was vital that one never be seen in public in the company of an adult. Indeed, that is precisely what made the Milky Way such a popular hangout; except for the mom and pop duo who ran the joint, it was an adult-free environment.

As Willie dragged me inside, I was hoping and praying that he would just order our milkshakes to go—but no, he was determined to turn the occasion into a tax deductible business lunch: burgers, milk shakes, fries—the works. As we sat waiting for our order to arrive, I shut my eyes and tried to make myself as small as possible.

"Poof, poof piffles." I muttered. "Make me just as small as Sniffles."

"What's that?" asked Willie. "Who did you say had syphilis?"

I sank still deeper into the Naugahyde.

"Not syphilis. *Sniffles*. It's the name of a character in a comic book. Mary Jane's mouse friend."

"Mary Jane has a mouse named Syphilis? Ha, that's rich!" Willie threw his head back and roared, so loudly that every pony and duck-tailed head in the place swiveled in our direction. I made myself even smaller—so small now that my flattop was level with the speckled Formica tabletop.

The conversation regarding Mary Jane and her syphilitic rodent friend continued for what seemed years, until finally Ilene arrived with my milkshake.

If nothing else had happened that Saturday, it still would have gone down as the worst day of my life. But no, there was more. Just when it appeared things couldn't possibly get worse, in walked my secret love Judy, flanked by her two girlfriends Linda and Susan. And as ill luck would have it, the trio settled into a banquette directly opposite the one occupied by Solicitor Willie and his incredible shrinking companion.

A tremor of fear rippled across the girls' faces when they saw Willie, whose rheumy gaze was firmly fixed upon their dimpled knees. Then came nervous giggles as they spotted me, cowering underneath the table. Susan whispered something into Linda's ear.

"Nice-looking girls!" Willie's voice boomed like a thunderclap, followed by a gentle rain of lettuce, onion and dill pickle fragments. "And if I'm not mistaken, that cute little brunette has her eye on you."

Willie was right. From the shadows, I could see that Judy was doing the very thing I'd been wishing and hoping and praying she'd do ever since Second Grade—she was actually making eye contact! But instead of the way I had dreamt it would happen—across a crowded room on some enchanted evening in a South Pacific paradise—it was happening on a sunlit afternoon at the Milky Way, a mediocre hamburger joint positioned at the ragged edge of an unremarkable galaxy.

Our "relationship" was never the same after that. Daydream as I might, I knew now that I'd never be the comic book superhero of *her* daydreams. Because what kind of hero cowers underneath tables like a shy little mouse? And hangs out with a dissipated sidekick named Willie?

CHAPTER SIX

THE LEAST YOU CAN BE IS A SAINT

For young men in other parts of the world, entering the priesthood is a life-defining event. But for the typical Mormon boy it's no big deal—at any rate, it wasn't a big deal as far as I was concerned. It didn't mean that I'd be required to read any holy books or serve an apprenticeship. I wouldn't need to wear holy vestments nor take a special vow. No, all I had to do was turn twelve, and then report to Bishop Smart's office for a "worthiness" interview.

The fact my brother Chuck had sailed through just such an interview three years earlier led me to expect no difficult questions would be asked—just the usual ones. Do I abstain from using tea, alcohol and tobacco? Do I support the leaders of the church? Do I pay a full tithe?

That last question would be the tricky one, for tithing had always been a sticking point in our family. After all, we were *poor Scots*. How could we be expected to hand over a tenth of our meager income to an institution already richer than General Motors?

No matter, I was fully prepared to answer in the affirmative. I'd done some calculating and determined that as an employee of the Deseret News, my take-home pay after expenses was *nothing*. Ten percent of nothing is nothing. *Ergo*, I was paying a full tithe.

So it came to pass that I was deemed worthy to receive the Aaronic Priesthood, and soon thereafter found myself encircled by older men wearing dark suits, half a dozen heavy hands resting upon my crew-cut scalp. A resonant voice from above pronounced me a deacon, which is the lowest rank of the lesser order of priesthood in the Mormon Church.

Which isn't to say I was exactly powerless, for according to the *Doctrine & Covenants* I'd just been handed "the keys to the ministering of angels." Should the spirit move me, I could drop to my knees at any time and place a call to the Other Side. I could lay my hands upon the brow of a sick person and command him to get well. The downside: I would now be expected to attend priesthood meetings.

Priesthood meetings got under way early on Sunday mornings, about the same time the Catholic priest across town was calling his parishioners to mass. It is purely a guy thing—no girls allowed, no Sister Brumwell on hand to establish the pitch and maintain the tempo during the opening hymn. Without her to guide us, we sounded like a bunch of unhappy farm animals.

After the braying died down, the ward clerk would rise to read the minutes of the previous meeting—I presume for the benefit of anyone who had missed out on the previous meeting. What he would have missed was the reading of the minutes from the Sunday preceding the previous Sunday. Thus, like an M. C.

Escher litho, priesthood meetings tended to go round and round and round ad infinitum.

Once the formal business had been disposed of, we'd disperse to our various classrooms. High priests would go upstairs to one room, priests and teachers to another. We lowly deacons would be herded into the basement. Our classroom was spare—four blank walls painted sea-foam green, rows of brown metal folding Samsonite chairs. Instead of a reliquary, we faced a blackboard. The absence of ornamentation was deliberate, in keeping with the Prophet Joseph Smith's disdain of everything Catholic.

Our instructor, Brother Talmadge, was an ordained elder—which is to say, a young man in his mid-twenties. His assignment: to instill in us a "testimony" regarding the restored gospel of Jesus Christ as it was revealed to Joseph Smith by the angel Moroni way back in the early nineteenth century. But first, there was roll call— Mormonism's version of call-and-response.

No institution outside of the military places more emphasis on record keeping than does the Mormon Church. Think of it as a way to measure righteousness, statistically. Whereas Muslims bow toward Mecca and Catholics recite the Rosary, devout Mormons bow down before bar graphs and pie charts. And flow charts. It's what I remember most from those Sunday morning sessions: Brother Talmadge drawing diagrams on the blackboard—lines connecting various circles and squares representing various high offices and lower levels of servitude. We were taught that there are three of just about everything: three figures in the godhead, three men in the first presidency of the church, three wandering

Nephites, three bases of sexual impropriety. (They seemed to correspond with what most teens called first, second, and third bases, though our teachers used terms less specific and less colorful.) Heaven consisted of three levels with a corporate structure much like that of the Beneficial Life Insurance Company, the only difference being that celestial executives wore white bathrobes instead of dark business suits.

Way down near the bottom of the cosmic organizational flow chart was a tiny cubicle representing us, the lowly deacons of the church. In the grand scheme of things we were definitely entry level personnel; however, if we kept our noses clean—and our shoulders to the wheel—we could expect to start moving up the corporate ladder, perhaps even *all the way up the ladder to the very top!* Brother Talmadge described the process as "eternal progression."

"As man is, God once was," he wrote on the blackboard. "As God is, man may become."

It was quite a carrot, one that would be dangled before my face time and again as I inched my way upward through the priesthood ranks. Not only might I one day become an angel in paradise, but I had a shot at becoming a god! Today a gangly kid perched upon a folding Samsonite chair, tomorrow a god on a golden throne, in charge of my very own planet!

I looked about the room. It was hard to imagine my fellow deacons as omnipotent overseers of worlds to come. Most of them had trouble staying awake in church, so how could they be expected to heed the prayers of multitudes? Not a one could grow a vegetable garden, let alone a Garden of Eden. And who among us could create a woman from a single rib. Not me—and I'd *tried*!

Then again, we were but twelve years of age. Perhaps such talents would evolve over time. For now, the important thing was to sit up straight, pay attention, and—above all—do exactly as we were told. Fellowship mattered, but *followship* mattered even more.

Newly empowered by the priesthood and a deity-in-waiting, in reality my main sacerdotal duty was to help pass round the bread and water during sacrament meetings. Partaking of the sacrament—was this still another variation on Catholicism? Absolutely not, according to Brother Talmadge. Catholics, he explained, embrace the concept of transubstantiation, believing that elements of the Eucharist become the blood and flesh of Christ. Moreover, their sacrament cups contain wine, which—even if it doesn't turn into blood—is against *our* religion.

What we deacons dished out on Sundays was just white bread crumbs and ordinary tap water. In our ward, as in all wards, the bread of choice was store-bought Wonder Bread. Not only is Wonder Bread white and delightsome, it's also enriched with twelve essential vitamins and minerals guaranteed to "build strong bodies twelve ways." Twelve is another of the church's extra-important numbers; no wonder that Wonder Bread is widely revered as Mormon manna.

Passing the sacrament entailed standing with heads bowed as the blessing was recited by one of two teenaged priests kneeling behind a table where the sacrament trays lay covered beneath a white tablecloth. To call the table a sacristy would be suggestive of Catholicism, and thus a sacrilege. Which is why, I suppose, we never called it anything but just the sacrament table. At the conclusion of the blessing, each of us would be handed a silver tray to pass around. Congregants helped by passing the tray from hand to hand the breadth of the pew. In theory, partaking of the sacrament signifies that one hasn't broken any of the major commandments, doesn't harbor heretical thoughts and supports the local bishop, his counselors and the general authorities of the church. In practice, *everyone* partakes. Why? *Because they are being closely watched by other members of the congregation.*

We deacons in particular were on the lookout for signs of unworthiness. No doubt about it, priestly empowerment is a heady experience for a twelve-year-old boy. Unfortunately, the feeling was fleeting, lasting only until the alarm clock rang the following Monday morning. For the remainder of the week, I was just another awkward middle schooler, in no position to look down upon *anyone*. At Carbondale Junior High, the empowered ones were athletic boys and their female counterparts, cheerleaders. I would have gladly traded my kingdom-to-come for just ten minutes of mortal glory on the playing field!

It wasn't as if I hadn't tried. Three years in a row I'd gone out for Little League and three years in a row I'd failed to make the cut. My big problem was a lack of self-confidence, which on the field, translated into a tendency to drop fly balls. It didn't help that I was routinely assigned to the outfield—not the best position for a boy who suffers from feelings of inadequacy.

At the conclusion of spring training, all who had tried out would assemble at the Carbondale civic auditorium, where team rosters would be announced. Names would be called, and one after another lucky boy would stride to the stage to accept his cap and uniform amid what sounded to my ears like thunderous applause.

As the festivities wound down, I would find myself still seated next to my mother, still waiting in vain for my name to be called. After three years of this, Mom could take it no longer. Rising to her feet, she announced she would never again accompany me to a Little League ceremony. "It's just too *humiliating*," she sniffed.

Is it any wonder then, that in years to follow, I would find myself turning more and more toward the church for love and acceptance? Compared to baseball, it was so much easier to succeed at Mormonism. I mean, here I was already a deacon at the age of twelve. In four short years I'd be a priest, and then an elder. Heck, the worst you could be was just a saint! And all I had to do in order to advance up the ranks was just show up. Simply by answering "here" whenever Brother Talmadge called the roll, I could accumulate a chestful of medals. Moreover, come summertime, there would be the free camping trip!

Priesthood camping trips were a ward tradition dating back to 1955—the year we ventured to Mesa Verde National Park. Billed as a reward for attending church regularly, it turned out to be the first of many times I'd be punished for being virtuous.

Transportation had been provided by Brother Bean, first counselor to Bishop Smart and owner of a small trucking company. So it came to pass that thirty young men and half a ton of camping gear were stuffed into the back of a moving van and shipped off

Virtue Is Its Own Punishment

to western Colorado. After a few hours of riding in total darkness, one of the brethren found a latch and managed to open the tailgate. As a result, we were able to enjoy a framed vista of sandstone cliffs and towering buttes as we passed through Moab. Unfortunately, facing backward in a moving vehicle while ingesting exhaust fumes tends to turn my stomach, so before long I was contributing splashes of green and yellow to the red rock palette of Utah's scenic Canyon lands.

By and by a, shoving match erupted. The combatants, one of whom was predictably my brother Chuck, bounced from one side of the van to the other, then tumbled end over end toward the open tailgate. Terrified that my brother was about to become road kill, I burst into tears—whereupon everyone called me a crybaby. I threw up again.

The van finally rolled to a stop somewhere in western Colorado. We set up camp beside a chocolate-colored river and rolled out our sleeping bags on the hard cold ground. My war surplus bag, stuffed with kapok, offered more weight than warmth. I had no air mattress, no pillow, nothing on which to rest my head and nothing to help settle my stomach. And absolutely no one to feel sorry for me!

Our hardships, Brother Talmadge was quick to point out, were practically pleasures in comparison to those endured by our pioneer forebears, who suffered not only physical discomforts but also the taunting of angry mobs back in Missouri. We were—that is, *I* was—advised to stop whining and be stalwart.

The following day we rolled into Gunnison, where we decided to go for a swim at the municipal swimming pool—and where, for the first time in my life, I was to feel the sting of religious persecution. No sooner had we emerged from the dressing room than the cry went up, "Here come the *Mormons!*" Whereupon, the locals scooted like a startled school of trout to the opposite end of the pool.

My brother Chuck was of a mind to knock some gentile heads together, but Brother Talmadge advised against it. Persecution, he explained, was a cross we'd just have to bear. Let the heathen rage; in the hereafter they'd learn the error of their ways and realize the correctness of ours. Then we shall even the score, but until then, pay them no mind. "Always remember," he added, "we *are* a peculiar people."

I did not enjoy being looked upon as peculiar, nor did my priesthood-holding companions. Yet the incident at Gunnison had a positive outcome in that it served to solidify our group. From that point on, we stopped fighting among ourselves and resolved to stand united against the anti-Mormon mobs, and—whenever possible—avoid non-Mormons altogether. The following night we "camped out" on the hardwood floor of a Mormon ward house. Our hosts seemed happy to have us.

The Colorado expedition was the first of many priesthood outings I would participate in, not all of which were ordeals. Some I remember fondly, in particular, fishing trips into the High Uinta Mountains in jeeps provided by Bishop Goodman.

By the mid-fifties the population of Carbondale had grown, so our ward was divided into two. Instead of the Fourth Ward, I now belonged to the Fifth. Jack Goodman was named bishop—the same Jack Goodman who owned Goodman Motors, the local Jeep dealership. This meant that instead of being transported across state lines in an airless moving van, we could now venture off the pavement into Utah's high country in four-wheel-drive vehicles.

There was just one catch: only those boys who maintained an 85 percent or better attendance record at priesthood meetings were eligible to participate. For me, that was incentive enough. During long dreary Sunday mornings, when scripture verses ran thick and the sea-foam green walls seemed to be closing in, I'd close my eyes and picture an Alpine lake mirroring stands of luminous aspen and pungent fir—glassy reflections dappled here and there by rising trout. On the blackboard, Brother Talmadge would be diagramming the various executive branches of the celestial kingdom; in my mind's eye, the interconnected circles were transformed into an aerial view of the Chain Lakes. Such blissful musings carried me through the winter, until the day of reckoning rolled round, when it was announced that I had achieved the top attendance record. Not that it much mattered, for at the last minute Bishop Goodman always relented, declaring that any boy who wished to go was welcome to tag along. Even Waldo Finn, who hadn't attended a single meeting, was invited. The more the merrier—that was Bishop Goodman's motto—and I suppose he was right, because Waldo, though surely destined to burn in hell later on, turned out to be the life of the party. In particular, I remember his inexhaustible stock of "werewolf" jokes—a variation of the knock-knock joke.

"Daddy, what's a werewolf?"

"Shut up and comb your face!"

In spite of the fact he never attended church—or perhaps because of it—Waldo was light years ahead of us developmentally. For instance, he professed to know what a virgin is—most likely because he'd been absent the day the subject had come up in priesthood meeting. The word had popped up in the course of a scripture reading, whereupon Rupert Ames had raised his hand and asked the teacher to define the term. Caught off guard, Brother Talmadge had been forced to improvise.

"Um ... a virgin is ... uh ... a woman who has never been *touched* by a man."

Fuzzy answers give rise to even fuzzier interpretations. Had the Virgin Mother never once bumped into a member of the opposite sex? I wondered. That time in the third grade when I not-so-accidentally brushed against the arm of my beloved Judy—had it been as good for her as it was for me?

Waldo laughed so hard the whole pup tent shook. "Don't you stupid morons know anything?" he asked. "Where have you *been* all your lives? Don't *tell* me you're all *virgins*?"

Well, of course we were. Not only were we virgins; we didn't even know the meaning of the word. Most of us would remain virgins for years to come, and one among us was destined to *die* a virgin. I often wonder whether Lieutenant Rupert Ames lamented that on the day he punched out of his crippled F-105 Thunderchief and fell to earth over North Vietnam, forever untouched and untouchable.

CHAPTER SEVEN

MISSING IN ACTION? NOT ME!

Years before the letters MIA became permanently affixed to his name on the Vietnam War Memorial, the whereabouts of Rupert Ames were never in doubt. Every Tuesday evening at seven o'clock I could find him at the ward house—him and all my other boyhood chums. Tuesday nights were reserved for Mutual or MIA—shorthand for Mutual Improvement Association. I loved Mutual, and never missed a single session.

    Although it took place in a church building, Mutual was nothing like church. It was more like Gymboree. Boys and girls attended, although there was precious little contact between the two. Girls customarily sat on the right-hand side of the chapel, boys on the left. At the conclusion of opening exercises, we'd disperse to separate classrooms. We boys would engage in Boy Scout activities while the girls would do whatever it is that young girls of that age do. So-called "MiaMaids," they could earn merit badges and advance in rank, all the way up to Golden Gleaner.

I thrived as a Boy Scout. Our troop went on hikes and camping trips, which in comparison to priesthood outings, were only mildly strenuous. Our scoutmaster Ray was an overgrown boy with no interest in nor possibility of ever advancing to a loftier office. Under his easygoing tutelage I learned how to blaze a forest trail, how to splint a broken leg, how to "whip" a rope, ditch a tent, and tie a bowline knot. In no time at all, I had advanced to the rank of Star—only two levels below Eagle. Were I to become an Eagle Scout, I knew I'd make my parents proud, especially my father.

Dad was an Eagle Scout, and rightly proud of it. He'd earned it the hard way, back before such badges were handed out like party favors. In 1925, he'd passed his swimming test by paddling across Emerald Lake, a glacial tarn that lies just below the summit of Mount Timpanogos. He never said as much, but I knew he remained hopeful that at least one of his three sons might follow in his hypothermic wake.

His best hope lay in perennial overachiever Jim, who in only two years, had advanced to the rank of Life—only one step below Eagle. But then he'd been offered a position as general manager of the local Safeway, where only months earlier he had started out as bag boy. So, at the tender age of fourteen, my oldest brother put childish things behind him.

Middle brother Chuck surprised everyone by advancing to Second Class, which is one step above Tenderfoot. At the court of honor, Mom had pinned his badge to his uniform upside down—custom dictating that it remain that way until such time as the recipient performs a good deed.

Three years later I inherited the family Scout uniform, Chuck's Second Class badge still affixed to the left shirt pocket—and *still* upside down. So now I was my father's last best hope, and I sensed I was walking in some pretty big shoes.

The uniform was plenty roomy as well. Mom had bought it extra-large, just in case one of her boys turned out to have a pituitary malfunction. As a result, whenever our troop went camping, I never needed to pack a tent—just poles.

My strong suit was knot tying, a skill for which I won blue ribbons at every camporee. My favorite knot was the bowline, which I had mastered thanks to a mnemonic trick: The rabbit pops out of its hole, runs around the tree, sees a fox and ducks back into its hole. From my father I'd learned knot-tying shortcuts, including how to turn two half hitches into a clove hitch, and how to transform three loops into a sheepshank.

One Tuesday evening out of the blue, a female runner appeared at troop headquarters bearing a note. The MiaMaids were learning to tie knots and had requested a demonstration. All hands pointed to me.

Giggling fits erupted as I stepped into the MiaMaid meeting room; evidently I was the first male ever to set foot inside that hallowed chamber. It was unsettling, but I drew a deep breath, whipped out my rope (more giggling) and proceeded to explain the difference between a square knot and a granny (*still* more tittering) knot.

What was it with these girls? I wondered. Surely they have no immediate plans to rig a mule pack, climb mountains or tether horses to a hitching post. I looked around. There were no animal skins tacked to the wall, no topographical maps of the High Uintas. Instead, there was a full color poster depicting the Mormon Temple in Salt Lake City—gray and granite spires piercing a cobalt blue sky. In the foreground, stood a MiaMaid, modestly attired in a blue jumper and white blouse, clutching a *Book of Mormon* to her breast. Next to it, a second poster showed the same young woman at a later date, this time seated on a velvet tuffet as she pens a letter. In a thought balloon above her pretty head hovers a young man, Pat Boone's identical twin.

In a third poster, the pair is shown standing side by side. Now she is dressed entirely in white, her hand resting lightly upon the young man's hand, which in turn rests upon a gilded doorknob affixed to an outsized door. The two are evidently about to enter the temple, there to be united in holy matrimony for "time and all eternity." Urging them inward is a crowd of Caucasian kinfolk of various ages, all beaming approvingly.

So now I understood the MiaMaids' interest in knots. They were learning how to rope and tie men!

Just about every Mormon girl I ever met followed the same "eternal" game plan. Attract a boy, send him on a mission, lock yourself away for two years until he returns, then throw the rope and drag him to the temple. Bear children, ideally six. Send your sons away on missions. Teach your daughter how to attract a boy. If he should try anything funny, send *him* on a mission!

MIA meetings generally lasted until eight o'clock, but the building remained open for another half hour or so. Ignoring the girls, we boys would make a beeline for the recreation hall, where we'd shoot baskets until the custodian turned out the lights.

At one end of the basketball court stood a small stage, normally curtained except whenever Sister Birkenstock, the ward drama director, was rehearsing a play. In which event, instead of playing basketball, I'd find myself performing in what is known as a "road show."

Road shows originated in pioneer times before the advent of radio and television. Cut off from the outside world, Latter-Day Saints had no choice but to entertain themselves. Thus out of necessity plowmen became playwrights; farm families spawned a slew of toothsome toddlers who would grow up (hopefully) to become the Osmonds. Yet for every Mormon performer who ever made it big in Branson, there are countless others, like me, who only succeeded in making fools of themselves in their hometown ward recreation halls.

That I should become a stage performer was inevitable, given Sister Birkenstock's conviction there is no such thing as a talentless child. Each and every one of us, she insisted—*if only we would put our minds to it*—could learn to sing, learn to dance, learn to deliver a line with conviction. No matter how shy and introverted, we could be taught to *emote!*

Some road shows were historical dramas set in pioneer days; others were morality plays set in the present, involving issues relevant to Victorian teenagers coming of age at the dawn of rock 'n' roll. Typically, the curtain would rise to reveal a cardboard facsimile of a malt shop. A motley gang of duck-tailed teens attired in black leather jackets is milling about the jukebox, grooving to the latest Elvis platter. An innocent young girl—invariably played by Sister Birkenstock's daughter Claudette—walks into the joint and settles on a stool at the soda fountain. She orders her usual: a plain vanilla milkshake. *To go.* But before she can go, the ringleader of the gang parks himself down on the stool next to hers.

"Hey, baby, what's up? Wanna go for a *ride*?"

The same basic storyline—essentially a remake of *Little Red Riding Hood*—such was the stuff of countless road shows, not to mention instructional films that were another staple of Tuesday nights. Produced by the Brigham Young University film department, they warned against keeping company with bad boys and girls. The moral in every case: Evil lurks in the hearts of *those who do not go to church*! (Italics theirs.) Non-churchgoing tempters and temptresses lurked around every corner but were particularly thick in pool halls and roadhouses.

It so happened that Carbondale had quite a few such establishments, each with its blacked-out windows and neon signs advertising BEER ON TAP. Having never set foot in one, I'd have had no idea what went on inside were it not for the BYU film department.

Roadhouses, I learned, are smoke-filled, dark, wretched hives of scum and villainy. The barmaid wears a low-cut blouse and has a bra strap showing. Her customers are leering, slavering *animals*. All smoke cigarettes, swill beer and speak fluent hepcat jive, pausing for breath only whenever the door swings open and in steps—Claudette Birkenstock!

Instantly, the gang springs into action, and next thing you know, Claudette has become woozy on 3.2 percent beer. At which point the ringleader steps forward and pops the golden question: "Hey, baby, wanna go for a ride?"

Whereupon, Claudette forgets all about the missionary-in-the-field she's been saving herself for and agrees to go for a thrill ride in a souped-up hotrod, which fails to negotiate Dead Man's Curve and ends up a smoldering wreck at the bottom of a ravine. Alas, poor Claudette—a casualty of the ongoing war between good and evil. As such, she joins a long list, including—according to The Book of Mormon—an entire race of pre-Colombian Native Americans known as Nephites.

Because the golden plates weren't illustrated, it's hard to know just what the vanished civilization looked like, so the BYU film department turned to secular sources for inspiration—specifically the epic Biblical sagas of Cecil B. DeMille. DeMille, in turn, had relied on the artistic vision of Arnold Friberg, a Utah painter whose muscular Moses looks to be a man who pumps stone tablets fifteen hours a day.

In addition to Hollywood storyboards, Friberg also produced illustrations for the *Book of Mormon*. According to Friberg, ancient America featured imposing stone fortresses with crenellated battlements from which pumped-up fair-skinned Nephites waged bloody battles against advancing hordes of "dark and loathsome" Lamanites.

Sooner or later in the life of every Mormon boy comes a day when he will be called upon to portray a Nephite warrior—unfortunately, without the benefit of Fribergian physique. Imagine Opie Taylor wearing Sheriff Andy's bathrobe, doing his adenoidal best to channel Charlton Heston, and you've got the picture.

Mercifully, road shows usually opened and closed on the same night; that is, unless the production elicited anything more than a smattering of parental applause, in which case it was deemed a runaway hit. Should that happen, you'd find yourself traipsing from ward house to ward house, night after night, declaiming the same lugubrious lines:

> I, Nephi, having been born of goodly parents, therefore I was taught somewhat in all the learning of my father; and having seen many afflictions in the course of my days, nevertheless, having been highly favored of the Lord in all my days; yea, having had a great knowledge of the goodness and the mysteries of God, therefore I make a record of my proceedings in my days.

Or, conversely: "Hey, baby, wanna go for a *ride*?"

CHAPTER EIGHT

AT PLAY IN THE BEET FIELDS OF THE LORD

Precisely when I began to turn into one of those "bad boys" that church leaders are forever warning young girls to stay away from, I can't say. All I can say with confidence is that I wish it had happened sooner. Had I known then what I know now, I wouldn't have merely fallen away—I would have jumped!

Alas, when one is a mere lad of thirteen or fourteen, it's not so easy to think straight, especially when everyone around you is telling you it's best if you *don't* think. Indeed, the only dissenting voice I ever heard when I was growing up was a still, small one that originated somewhere inside my head. I'm pretty sure it wasn't the Holy Ghost speaking.

The first time I heard it, I was daydreaming my way through another priesthood meeting, counting leaping trout as Brother Talmadge droned on about the importance of baptism by complete submersion—

as opposed to the wrongheaded Catholic practice of sprinkling. The still, small voice inside piped up: "Hey, isn't this a lot like those never-ending quarrels Terry and I used to have regarding which movie actor is the one and only king of the cowboys?"

It so happened there were a number of Catholic families living in Carbondale. Some were my neighbors, and as far as I could tell, none worshipped the devil. The Catholic kids I knew attended the Catholic Church for just one reason: because their *parents* were Catholic. And so why was I sitting here in Brother Talmadge's deacon quorum? Because *my parents* were Mormons.

It occurred to me that religion isn't so much a choice as it is an inherited trait. So why should we take such pride in what we are, or labor so diligently to convert others to our way of thinking, our method of baptism?

I never voiced such thoughts to anyone—how could I? There was no such thing in our meetings as an open discussion—only pat answers offered in response to canned questions gleaned from the official lesson plan. We never cracked open a non-Mormon book, not when all we ever needed to know was contained in Bruce R. McConkie's *Mormon Doctrine*. And if we couldn't find what we were looking for there, well, we could do as Brother Talmadge advised: Fall upon your knees and *pray* for an answer—same as the prophet Joseph Smith had done when *he* was in doubt. Pray with an open mind and a pure heart and the answer will come in the form of "a burning in the bosom." And when the burning subsides, you will know for certain that there is but one true church on the face of the earth. *Ours.* End of discussion.

In any event, I wasn't of a mind to stir up trouble. It was just so much easier to go with the flow and do whatever was asked of me. Do exactly as told, and reap the benefits of brotherhood. I enjoyed the camaraderie, the scouting outings, the fishing trips, and basketball. Heck, I almost even enjoyed assign-ments to the church farm, which lay just south of the Carbondale city limits. The cash crop there was sugar beets, proceeds from which went to feed and clothe needy members. Farming was healthy exercise and interesting—at least for the first five or so minutes.

Early in the springtime, about an hour before sunup, the various quorums would assemble in the beet field. Following a brief word of prayer, each man and boy would be issued a short-handled hoe and assigned a row of sugar beet seedlings. Owing to the curvature of the earth, I could never quite see to the far end of my assigned row.

Bending low, I'd start out—swinging my hoe from side to side in order to thin the seedlings. In the unlikely event I should ever come to the end of my row, I was to move over to the next one and start working my way back.

Around noontime I'd hear the faint clanging of a dinner bell. My fellow beet thinners also heard it; in unison, we'd drop our hoes and race toward the cookhouse. There we'd find a table laden with a platter of sloppy joe sandwiches, a huge bowl of potato salad, molded mounds of quivering green Jell-O, pans of lemon-frosted carrot cake, and a tuna fish and loaf casserole sufficient to feed a hungry multitude. It was a miracle wrought by the women's auxiliary branch of the church, without which the big wheels of Mormondom would soon grind to a shuddering halt.

On call 24 hours a day, Relief Society sisters cater weddings and funerals, comfort the bereaved, visit the sick, and run errands for shut-ins. Once a month, each housewife in the ward will answer the doorbell to find a pair of Relief Society sisters known as "visiting teachers."

Should a frazzled homemaker fall behind in her chores, an entire brigade of sisters bearing mops and brooms will converge on her doorstep.

Since pioneer days, the Relief Society has been vital to the workings of the church because—truth be told—Mormon men are basically helpless. They can't cook, they can't sew, they can't clean house, and they can't help raise children. Basically all Mormon men can do is attend meetings and issue proclamations. Back when they were farmers, they frequently set off in search of more converts—in which case it fell to the womenfolk to keep the farm going. And as the farm grew, the man who was seldom around the house would go abroad again in search of additional wives, aka fieldhands.

Come September, it was time to harvest the sugar beets, which by now had grown to be gigantic tubers weighing five to fifteen pounds each. Instead of a short-handled hoe, I wielded a wicked-looking implement that resembled a machete, except that it had a curved spike at the end of the blade. The idea was to hook the beet with the spike, lop off its top and then toss it into the bed of a truck. The truck's bed had high staked sides, so heaving the beets required considerable effort. And because no two beets weighed the same, it was hard to judge just how much effort was required. An average-sized beet could be lobbed like a basketball, while a larger one might demand a shot-put technique. Problem was, none of us were skilled shot putters. I'd heave a monster beet heavenward hard as I could and hope it would land in the bed of the pickup. But if it came down on the far side of the truck, you'd hear a sickening *thud,* followed by a groan. Presently a beet about the same size would come falling from the sky.

For those of us who escaped permanent brain injury, church farming was a fun outing, one that brought together men and boys in a sort of patriarchal apprenticeship. The idea was that eventually the boys would settle down, stop goofing off and become serious. Because Mormonism is nothing, if not serious.

The very best way to wipe the grin off the face of a young man is to yoke him to an older man whose idea of a good time is knocking on the doors of people who, by and large, would prefer to be left alone. The activity was called ward teaching.

Each ward teaching team consisted of an adult male and a junior companion; their assignment, to visit every month a selected number of church members residing within the boundaries of the ward. Their mission, as set forth in the *Doctrine & Covenants,* was to "visit the house of each member, exhorting them to pray vocally and in secret and attend to all family duties ... and see that there is no iniquity in the church, neither hardness with each other, neither lying, backbiting, nor evil speaking."

Ward teaching was a bit like tracting with Willie the Solicitor—except that my senior partner, Elder Boorman, was sobriety personified. Also, because the people on our route were all listed as members on the church rolls, they couldn't very well slam their doors in our faces. No, they were duty bound to at least *pretend* to be glad to see us.

I don't recall doing much in the way of praying or exhorting, though. For the most part, ward teaching consisted of idle chitchat, and not until it was time to leave would Elder Boorman suddenly remember that we were on official church business—at which point he'd pull out the lesson manual, clear his throat and read the monthly message as prescribed by the presiding General Authorities. Then he would turn to me.

"Is there anything you'd like to add, Richard?"

I could never think of anything. "Amen to what you said," I said.

We'd all stand and bow our heads and pretend to close our eyes. Brother Boorman would invoke the Lord's blessings upon whichever household we were in. Then it was off to the next address on our list. If we were lucky, it would be the home of an *active* member of the ward and not someone like Romney Usher. Brother Usher *never* went to church; just knocking on his door filled me with dread.

What was strange about Romney Usher was that he carried on as if it didn't matter a whit what the ward teachers might think of him. His living room looked nothing like those we were accustomed to; it looked entirely too *lived in*. There were books and magazines and newspapers strewn about, and a reading lamp positioned in such a way that one might actually be able to read by it. The sofa was worn and bore a telltale indentation suggesting that someone had sat on it. There were no church books on display and the pictures on the wall were not of Mormon temples and church officials. There were unfamiliar odors in the air. Tobacco? Coffee? Beer? My nose began to twitch. I was like a bloodhound on the scent.

Many times when we came calling, Romney wouldn't bother to turn off the television or even unrecline his reclining chair. He'd just lie there, semi-horizontal, in his pajama bottoms and tattered undershirt.

So-called "inactive" Mormons such as Romney Usher constitute a surprisingly large percentage of the church's membership. A big part of ward teaching entails trying to pry them from their La-Z-Boys and reinstall them on hardwood pews. It's a daunting, thankless task. If exhorting, praying and preaching failed to reactivate the dormant Saint, we'd switch to the Dale Carnegie approach; that is, we'd try to figure out what the backslider's interests were and pretend to be interested in those. We'd take note of the pictures on the walls, the books in the bookcase and the magazines on the coffee table. If the subject was watching—or *trying* to watch—a sporting event on television, we'd talk sports.

"What's that you're watching?" we'd ask. "World Series? Dodgers and Yankees? Seventh game, you say? *Bottom* of the ninth? What's the score? Tied? No kidding. Who's up? Mantle? Say, that reminds me—the *Senior M Men* play softball every Wednesday evening at six. We could sure use an extra glove if you'd care to join us ...."

So-called "fellowshipping" rarely worked on members as resolutely inactive as Romney Usher. It was more effective in drawing young people into the fold—in particular, if the ward house were home to the only Boy Scout troop or basketball court in town. Even parents averse to religion will often permit their children to participate in certain church activities. They figure it's preferable to a honky-tonk roadhouse with all the attendant risks.

What I learned from ward teaching is the importance of home décor as a barometer of saintliness. No matter what the rest of the house might look like, it's vital that the living room be in apple pie order. The walls and carpet should be off-white and the curtains of semi-transparent material like the diaphanous raiment of angels. Like the unused room in the Salt Lake Temple that is reserved for the second coming of the Savior, the unlived-in living room of a proper Mormon household is reserved for church visitors. By way of artwork, you can't go wrong with anything involving the founder Joseph Smith and/or current church apostles. There shall be no books or periodicals on display except those penned by Mormon authors with middle initials and published under ecclesiastical supervision. Prominently dis-played upon the coffee table will be the three holy books comprising the so-called concordance: *The Book of Mormon, The Pearl of Great Price,* and *The Doctrine & Covenants.* And, needless to say, it's *not* called a *coffee* table.

Our own house was different. Owing to a shortage of space, we were forced to live in the living room. So when the home teachers came calling, my mother would quickly gather up the scattered newspapers, magazines, coffee cups and playing cards. My father would pull on his socks and shoes and adjust his recliner to full upright. The dog would be exiled to the basement. Then we'd all do our best to emulate a page torn from *The Improvement Era.*

Were my parents hypocrites? Or were they just trying their best to keep up appearances? If so, they weren't doing a very good job of it, and because they weren't doing a very good job of it, it was a safe bet that my father would never be called to serve in the bishopric, nor would my mother be named Relief Society president. On the righteousness scale, we just weren't cutting it.

In order to rise to a position of prominence in the church, or even to wear a tiara and ride on a float in the annual Days of 47 Parade, one must be descended from pioneers who crossed the plains afoot or in covered wagons. Alas, our ancestors had come to Utah not pulling handcarts but pushing ore carts. They were coal miners, and coal mining just doesn't lend itself to righteousness.

Mom hadn't been raised Mormon and wasn't baptized until she was in her mid-forties. It hadn't stopped her from drinking coffee and tea. My father, too, drank coffee and tea, and although none of us kids were supposed to know about it, he also smoked cigarettes.

The ritual went like this: Each night, just before bedtime, Dad would announce that he was stepping outside to "lock the car." Ten minutes later he'd return, smelling strongly of tobacco. I'm sure Mom was aware of his habit, because once my brother Chuck popped open the glove box of our 1950 Mercury and a pack of Camel cigarettes fell out.

"Hey cool!" my brother exclaimed. "Cigarettes!"

"Put those back!" Mom snapped. "They belong to a friend of your father's."

So if Mom knew, and we kids also knew, then why didn't Dad just come clean? I suspect he didn't want his sons to follow his example and take up the unhealthy habit. And yet it came to pass, in the fullness of time, that I became a smoker. However, I took great pains never to light up in front of my father, who by that time had kicked the habit. So in a way, I suppose you could say I was setting a good example for him, same as he once did for me.

CHAPTER NINE

THERE'S A PLACE IN FRANCE

As a boy, I spent more time than is considered normal wandering the foothills by myself. The fact our house sat near the edge of a vast unpeopled wilderness presented a temptation I simply couldn't resist; thus, at every opportunity I'd reach for my Red Ryder signature air rifle, whistle for my springer spaniel, Elmer, and head for the hills. As long as I was packing a firearm, the good citizens of Carbondale never worried about what deviltry I might be up to.

One city block from our back doorstep, lawns gave way to sagebrush, pavement to a network of wild game trails. The official city limit was marked by a debris field consisting of empty beer cans, whiskey and wine bottles, cigarette butts, girlie magazines and spent condoms. Prohibition makes litterbugs of us all.

Presently I'd arrive at the familiar mesa we knew as Wood Hill, beyond which lay a taller mesa my friends and I had christened Mystery Mountain. Higher still rose the distant Book Cliffs—better known locally as the Blue Mountains. Thus in Carbondale, as in heaven, there were three separate tiers of glory.

My two older brothers had never ventured beyond the first level, and they hadn't been there long before one of them spied a snake in the brush and sounded the alarm. A dozen of us had fled Wood Hill that day, leaving behind a roaring campfire and at least five dollars' worth of groceries. Bringing up the rear of the thundering herd was me, afraid to look back lest I come face to face with the pursuing serpent.

My brothers never went back, but I did. Time and again I crisscrossed the mesa in search of our hastily abandoned campsite, but never found it. I concluded it must have gone the way of the Dutchman's mine, Hirohito's sword, and Joseph Smith's golden plates.

One day I happened upon what we knew as a blow snake, but instead of chasing after me, it just lay there. It didn't scare me a bit, nor did the snowy owl that swooped, phantomlike, within inches of my head late one afternoon. The badger Elmer cornered in a hole *did* scare me; however, I found that if I simply backed away, the badger was more than happy to see me go.

In time, I came to feel very much at home on Wood Hill. Many a happy hour I spent stretched out, lizardlike, on a warm bed of sandstone. I'd gaze into the deep blue firmament and wonder what lay beyond. I sometimes wondered why no one else in my little town ever did the same. Heaven knows there was no shortage of rocks to sit on, and no end to the sky. Yet the good citizens of Carbondale preferred their rectangular lots and manicured lawns. None ever ventured into the wilds except in large, boisterous groups.

Virtue Is Its Own Punishment

From the east came the sound of sporadic gunfire. It being Saturday, I surmised it must be Rocky Rockwell's Army blazing a path of destruction across Clark's Valley. Many jackrabbits would die before the day was out, and only Brother Rockwell would know the reason why.

Rocky Rockwell was a seminary teacher—as close to a professional clergyman as can be found in the Mormon Church. His classroom, in a building planted right next door to Carbondale High, was where religious courses were taught during regular school hours. Next door to each and every public high school throughout Utah stands a Mormon seminary, its purpose to ensure that the separation between church and state never grows to more than just a few silly millimeters.

Students who don't wish to attend seminary are free to spend the hour known as "released time" doing something else—for instance, sneaking off to the nearest honky-tonk roadhouse for a quick drink and a cigarette, followed by a joy ride in a stolen car resulting in the obligatory fatal crash.

Considering the alternative, my parents insisted I sign up for seminary. I didn't mind because a lot of attractive young women also attended seminary.

Brother Rockwell enjoyed a reputation as Carbondale's warmest and most loving human being, a man endowed with a heart so pure and tender that just about *anything* would cause tears to well up in his eyes and a catch to form in his throat. And it's common knowledge that whenever a Mormon male breaks into tears, you just *know* that he's sincere.

A typical seminary session would begin with an opening prayer delivered by a student volunteer.

Almost always, that volunteer was Claudette Birkenstock. Claudette prayed that the spirit of the Holy Ghost would be with us for the duration of the period, and that Brother Rockwell would be granted "the spirit in order that whatsoever he might sayeth unto us would strengthen and nourish our testimonies. In the name of Jesus Christ, amen."

What the hell was going on with Claudette? I wondered. Was she developing a lisp? Speaking in tongues? Or was she herself possessed of "the spirit?"

What*ever*—asking the Holy Spirit to abide with Brother Rockwell was like hauling coals to Newcastle. He differed from all the other Mormon men in town in that he employed his "church voice" not only on Sundays but *all the time.*

Bother Rockwell would begin with a reading from the pages of the *Book of Mormon,* but wouldn't get far before his voice would begin to crack and his eyes teared up. I'd think, "*Uh-oh, here comes still another flashback to his missionary days in Paris, France.*

That Rocky Rockwell should be called to serve a mission to Paris is the strongest argument I can think of against Albert Einstein's dictum that God doesn't play dice with the universe. In an orderly universe, God would have called Rocky to serve in Paris, *Idaho.* There he would have fit in and wouldn't have been subjected to two and one-half long years of unrelenting rejection, tempered by one libidinous come-on.

The French, Brother Rockwell explained, are a people in desperate need of salvation. Wine, women, song, abstract art, old cheese, crusty bread—there was simply no end to the decadence. Everywhere he went he was confronted by towering cathedrals, ornate stone monuments to the great and abominable church of the devil. On the steps of Notre Dame he was jeered by hecklers, menaced by gargoyles. Along the banks of the Seine he'd been shocked by the sight of young lovers shamelessly embracing. Threading a camel through the eye of a needle would be *easy* compared to converting a Parisian to Mormonism, he said. The French were just unbearable!

I suspected at least one Frenchman might have had the same opinion of Brother Rockwell, whose nose angled off to one side. But getting punched in the nose hadn't been the worst of it, not by a long shot. No, the worst thing to befall Brother Rockwell during his sojourn in Paris was being propositioned by a young French girl.

"She was, well, I suppose you could say she was just *desperate*," he declared. "She would have done *anything* to get to America."

For those of us whose minds had been elsewhere, Rocky now had our undivided attention.

The crisis occurred after Rocky had gone to Francine's apartment expecting to be introduced to her mother and father, only to find out that Francine's parents were nowhere in sight. Undaunted, he and his stalwart companion set up their flannel board and launched into "The First Discussion."

At the mention of the companion, my interest flagged somewhat. I'd forgotten that Mormon missionaries *always* travel in pairs, the idea being that temptation is greatest when no one is watching. Then again, things might be different in Paris, France. Perhaps what Francine had in mind was a *ménage a trois*.

The following evening, the predatory *femme fatale* somehow managed to lure Brother Rockwell back to her apartment, sans companion, for what he thought was going to be "The Second Discussion." But no, that's not what she had in mind.

To my infinite disappointment, that's as far as the story ever went. No matter how many times Brother Rockwell retold it, it always ended the same. The farthest he would go down the road to explicitness was to say that Francine was willing to *do anything* in order to get to America. Those of us in the audience were left to fill in the blanks, and fill them in we did.

Unwilling to sacrifice his virginity, Brother Rockwell had failed to convert even a single French person. There was just something about the French, he said, a certain *resistance*.

"I never could get through to 'em," he said, voice cracking with unpent emotion. "God bless 'em, but they're *stubborn*. So many times I felt like reaching out and, and ..."

Brother Rockwell's right arm began moving up and down in a chopping motion "Gosh dang it! So many times I was tempted to just knock some frog upside the head with a baseball bat!"

Frenchmen weren't the only targets of Brother Rockwell's wrath. Also deserving of a few whacks were the sex fiends who routinely—according to his telling—take advantage of innocent Mormon schoolgirls, not to mention those gentile mobs that had gang-raped Mormon womenfolk on church pews back in Nauvoo. Lastly, there was the sound thrashing that awaited the first man who had the temerity to lay hands on Brother Rockwell's wife.

But who had designs on Sister Rockwell? I had looked upon the woman, but never with lust in my heart. She was plain and slump-shouldered with a hangdog look in her eyes—as if someone had threatened to bash her with a baseball bat.

When Friday rolled around, Brother Rockwell's mood would brighten a bit as he contemplated the weekend. Saturday was the day he went rabbit hunting.

"Yes, I understand they are furry and cute," he explained. "But God bless 'em, they *are* a problem."

Just what the problem was, he never did say. Perhaps, like the communists and the Catholics, the jackrabbits of Clark Valley were out to take over the world. Or maybe, just maybe, they were just itching to lay their furry little paws on *Sister Rockwell!*

Brother Rockwell's arm had resumed making that chopping motion. The rabbit "problem" had gotten so bad, he said, that it was more than just one seminarian armed with a .22-caliber rifle could manage. All able-bodied young men who wished to join in the hunt were invited to meet in front of the seminary at eight a.m. sharp. BYOB. Bring Your Own Bullets.

I never participated in Brother Rockwell's crusade to rid the county of jackrabbits, but many of my classmates did, and from what they told me, I gather it was a bloody affair, with many rounds fired and hundreds of rabbits dispatched to the hereafter, without a single tear being shed on their behalf. How could that possibly be?

Itzhak Fried of UCLA's Brain Institute writes of Syndrome E, the "cognitive fracture" that permits killers to distance themselves from their evil deeds. It's a phenomenon that made possible the Holocaust and subsequent genocides in Rwanda, Cambodia and Bosnia. Cognitive fracturing has also occurred in the Utah Territory, where in 1857 the Fancher Party, consisting of 122 non-Mormon emigrants from Arkansas, was ambushed and massacred by Mormon militiamen posing as Indians.

Of course, we never discussed the so-called Mountain Meadows Massacre in seminary class. However, I distinctly remember a time, a warm moonlit night in August, 1958, when Syndrome E suddenly reared its ugly head.

It happened along State Route 191, which runs through Indian Canyon between Duschesne and Carbondale. A quorum of young priesthood holders were on their way home from a fishing trip into the High Uintas late at night, when the headlamps of our pickup illuminated a roly-poly form lumbering across the road as fast as its little legs could carry it. Brother Talmadge immediately slammed on the brakes and ordered us to pile out of the truck bed.

"Get it, Get it!" He shouted. Get it? Get *what*?

"The porcupine!" Brother Talmadge exclaimed. "Quick, before it gets away!"

One of the frontrunners succeeded in heading the porcupine off and turning it back onto the roadway, into the glare of the headlamps. Then came a sickening thump as one of our party fetched the animal a blow across the back.

"The nose!" I heard Brother Talmadge shout. "Hit it in the *nose*. Bash its *face* in!"

We all set about doing as we were told. I searched the shrubbery until I found a suitable stick, and then took careful aim at a spot between the cowering porcupine's coal black eyes. *Crunch!*

"Good *work*!" exclaimed Brother Talmadge.

Several blows followed, until at last the porcupine lay still, a steaming corpse growing cold beneath a star-spangled sky. Clutching our bloody cudgels, we boys paused to admire our handiwork. Then Brother Talmadge kicked the carcass into the barrow pit and ordered us all back into the truck. Tomorrow would be a Sunday, and we had to rise early in time for church.

CHAPTER TEN

A MARVELOUS WORK AND WONDER BREAD

I was now sixteen years old and moving steadily up the priesthood ranks. From deacon I had advanced to teacher, and now I was on the verge of being ordained a priest. Of course I'd be spending no time in divinity school, nor would I be required to don special vestments. I *would* be expected to remain celibate, which in my case was a no-brainer.

Essentially, all that was required was a good attendance record, plus I'd have to undergo a brief oral examination in the bishop's office. I was confident I'd pass, for by now I knew what sort of questions to expect. For instance, I knew the questions would be phrased in the present tense. Thus, should the bishop ask if I pay a full tithe, I could answer in the affirmative without crossing my fingers. The fact I'd only just begun paying and would stop tomorrow wasn't anything the bishop needed to know. And should he discover at a later date that I had stopped paying my dues, there was no chance I'd be busted to a lower rank. In the entire history of the church only one member, Elijah Abel, had been booted out of the priesthood—the result of a background check that revealed Abel was of African ancestry. Negro blood, even a single drop, was the only thing that could hold me back. Just *why* it should be so had been covered time and again in the classroom. No matter—it was still confusing.

According to Mormon doctrine, the Negro "problem" originated in the pre-existence, at a time when one third of God's spirit children staged an uprising. In the war that ensued, the rebellious faction was defeated and cast out of heaven—along with their leader Lucifer.

The triumphant two-thirds had fought alongside God's favorite son Jesus Christ. However, not all of them received honorable discharges, fully half having conducted themselves on the celestial battlefield in a manner described as "less valiant." When such insufficiently valiant spirits are sent down to earth, they are born into the lineage of Cain and bear the "curse" of a dark skin.

Curiously, no questions were ever raised in priesthood class. I mean, a *war*—in *heaven*? How might such a war be waged, and with what manner of weaponry? How does one kill or even wound an immortal adversary?

Of course, racial discrimination was commonplace in the 1950s and relatively frictionless in Carbondale, where dwelled but one black family, the Wellingtons. Nonetheless, it wasn't a good idea to belittle a Wellington kid in person, because all were of sturdy stature and not the least bit lacking in valor. Willie Wellington, for example, played point guard on our high school basketball team, and it took at least two Caucasian defenders to stop him from scoring in the lane. Willie had distinguished himself on the baseball diamond and football field as well. Matter of fact, if not for Willie Wellington, the Carbondale high school trophy case would be bare as Mother Hubbard's cupboard.

Two decades would pass before church leaders, feeling heat from the Civil Rights Movement and under pressure to improve BYU's running game, would finally lift the sanction against dark-skinned people. No matter, the Wellingtons of Carbondale remained devout Baptists.

If *anyone* had demonstrated a lack of valiance in those days before the 1978 "revelation," it was *me*. If I'd had an ounce of backbone or even a lick of sense, I would have spoken out. I would have stood up and denounced church doctrine for the racist nonsense it obviously was. Regrettably, because of the way I'd been carefully taught, I had neither brains nor courage. I was completely unaware of the civil rights movement. The freedom riders weren't coming to Utah, so why worry? I wasn't black; I was white like Nephi—and on top of everything else, a *priest*!

Priests got to do important stuff; for instance, it was our job to bless the sacrament at Sacrament Meetings, which meant we got to sit up front on the same level as the organist, on chairs facing the congregation. This put us on a level close to that of General Authorities, who get to sit in padded chairs facing the congregation during general conference sessions in the Salt Lake Tabernacle.

Following the opening prayer and singing of the sacrament hymn, all eyes would shift to the priests as we knelt to consecrate the Wonder Bread crumbs and trays of tiny paper cups filled with chlorinated tap water. Unlike most Mormon prayers, the sacrament blessing is short and the wording prescribed. For our convenience, the blessing was printed on a three-by-five-inch card, and we had been advised beforehand that were we to stumble upon a word, we were to stop immediately and start over from the beginning. Like the Miranda warning, the blessing wasn't legally binding unless you read it just right.

One Sunday as I knelt before the sacrament table, reading the blessing off the cue card, I spotted a typographical error:

> O God, the Eternal Father, we ask thee in the name of thy Son, Jesus Christ, to bless and sanctify this bread to the souls of all those who partake of it, that they may eat in remembrance of the body of thy Son, and witness unto thee, O God, the Eternal Father, that they are willing to take upon them the name of thy Son, and always *remeber* Him and keep His commandments....

I read the word as "remember;" however, soon as the deacons had taken away the trays, I nudged my fellow priest Sven Jensen in the ribs. "I think I messed up, Sven," I whispered. "According to what it says on the card, we're supposed to *remeber* Him."

Over the course of the next several Sundays, I repeatedly challenged Sven to read the blessing *exactly* as written. He repeatedly declined. So finally I accused him of being an insufficiently valiant coward, at which point he took offense. Sven was anything but a coward, and to prove it, the following Sunday he knelt before the sacrament table and in a booming voice reminiscent of Gabriel Heatter recited the card verbatim. No sooner had the word "remeber" escaped his lips than the bishop sprang from his padded chair and rushed over.

"You didn't read it right," he whispered into Sven's ear. "You'll have to start over."

"Yes, I *did* read it right," Sven whispered back. "See for yourself." Sven held up the cue card and pointed to the misspelling.

The bishop wasn't amused, and after church let out, summoned me to his office for an impromptu counseling session.

"Richard," he began, "I have a favor to ask. I've always considered you a natural born leader. I have a hunch whichever way you decide to go, the other boys in the quorum will follow. But a boy like Jensen, he's impressionable. He's weak-minded and susceptible to promptings of the Devil. So what I'm asking is, would you do me a big favor and keep a close eye on him? See that from now on, he toes the line."

Thus began my long and tortured relationship with Bishop Orrin Snarr. No one ever worked harder to steer this young boy straight than Snarr did, and with such little success. Even today, whenever he hears my name spoken, he shudders. "Richard seemed to hold so much promise," he laments. "It's a shame he never amounted to anything."

Orrin Snarr was our recently anointed bishop, a newcomer to the ward and a newcomer to Carbondale as well. An optometrist by trade, he'd come down from Utah County, determined to help the folks of

Carbondale to see better and—better still—see the light. What he'd found wasn't encouraging. Although geographically situated inside the Beehive state, Carbondale was a world apart, culturally. What to make of a brothel operating in plain sight, of saloons that openly defied state liquor laws by brazenly dispensing mixed drinks? And how is it that only Democrats are elected to public office? Orrin Snarr was a stranger in a strange land. However, once he'd gotten settled in and become acquainted with some of the resident religious fanatics—i.e., Brother Rockwell, Snarr began to take heart. Perhaps among the goats there were sheep to be saved; all they needed was a right-thinking optometrist to show them the way.

In no time at all, Orrin Snarr moved up the ecclesiastical ranks and within a year of his arrival was named bishop of the Carbondale Fifth Ward. From the outset, he made it clear he wasn't pleased with the *laissez-faire* management style of his predecessors. For instance, the practice of allowing just anyone to join priesthood outings into the High Uintas, when the rules specifically stated that only those boys maintaining an 85% or better attendance record are eligible. From now on, he declared, the rules would be strictly enforced! Yet attendance levels stayed about the same, and when finally summer rolled around only two boys had qualified—Barney Brown and me. It was the smallest expedition ever, and the least enjoyable. There were no late night pup tent bull sessions, no werewolf jokes, no canned bean bombs exploding in the campfire. During the day there was no one to talk to except our adult leader, and nothing much we wanted to hear from him.

No matter, Bishop Snarr didn't care whether the trip was no fun. He made it clear that we weren't placed on this earth merely to sit around campfires roasting marshmallows and telling werewolf jokes. No, we had been sent to earth for a *purpose*, that *purpose* being to *magnify* our calling as priests in the church and to prepare ourselves for the rapidly approaching day when we would be called on missions and sent forth into the world to preach the gospel.

The way Orrin Snarr saw it, going on a mission wasn't an option; it was something *we had to do*. A Mormon male who hadn't served his two years in the mission field would be like a soldier who hadn't undergone basic training. How could he call himself a Saint if he hadn't undergone the secret temple initiation? How could he become a member in good standing if he didn't wear the holy undergarments? If he hadn't spent two years of his young life peddling the gospel door-to-door, how could he ever be considered virtuous?

The more I listened to Bishop Snarr, the more I began to realize that every church activity in which I had participated had been steering in just one direction. Before Orrin Snarr came along, I'd *thought* about serving a mission, but only in the abstract. I might or might not answer the call, depending upon whether or not it sounded like something I might actually want to do. But now I was being told that missionary service was the right thing to do even if I didn't want to do it. Serving a mission was a necessary rite-of-passage, one that would lead me to "a higher understanding" of what it means to be a Mormon.

I felt not the slightest desire to preach—still, there were aspects of missionary service that appealed to me. Wouldn't it be nice to be looked up to? To be not merely accepted, but *venerated*.

Behold the newly-returned missionary! Why, only two years earlier he was naught but a pimple-pocked, disorganized adolescent. But look at him now: clean-shaven, ramrod straight, fluent in a foreign language and brimming with tales of *fantastic* adventures in some faraway land.

Whenever a young Mormon comes home from the mission field, it's like the night Lucky Lindy touched down in France. At the airport, he's mobbed by well-wishers, smothered with kisses, hugged half to death by his parents and grandparents, siblings, aunts, uncles, cousins, neighbors—just about everyone except that "special" girl he'd left behind, the one who had promised to wait for him but hadn't specified for how long. But no matter; there's never a shortage of comely young women eager to take up with a returned missionary. Come Sunday evening, they can be seen jockeying for positions on the front pew, eager to get a close look at the conquering hero.

"G'day, mates," he might begin. Or, "Buenas noches hermanos y hermanas." Or, "Howdy, y'all." The idea being to dazzle the flock with his newfound command of some exotic vernacular.

Presently he will launch into the meaty part of his homecoming speech, telling of various and sundry *fantastic* experiences and of how, as a result of two years spent knocking on doors, his testimony as to the truthfulness of the restored gospel has grown and grown. In conclusion, he will express his humble gratitude to those members of the ward who sent letters of encouragement while he labored abroad and to those who contributed financially to his upkeep. All the while, he will be wondering whatever became of the girl who promised to wait.

In the days following his triumphant return, the returned missionary is a much sought guest speaker at informal get-togethers known as firesides. Such meetings are for young people and take place not in the ward house but in the living rooms of private homes under close parental supervision. The returned missionary might begin his presentation by showing off a few of the foreign words he'd picked up in the course of his travels, words such as "*Nyet, nein, adios, adieu, bon giorno.*" Then it was on to the slide show, a Kodachrome glimpse into the demon-infested world that lurked on the far side of Zion's sheltering hills. First, a still of the missionary and his constant companion posing stiffly on a tropical beach, wearing dark suits, white shirts and narrow neckties while semi-naked natives frolicked in the background. Click forward to a picture of the one-room daub-and-wattle chapel the elders had constructed with help from a recent convert eclectically attired in a floral print lava-lava topped with a charcoal-gray sport coat. Half Polynesian, half polyester.

Neckties and dark suits notwithstanding, it looked to be a pretty nice posting—a refreshing contrast to the dull gray hills of Carbondale. The more color slides I saw, the more I began to dream of escaping to some faraway tropical paradise. Which may explain why, the first time I set eyes on her, I fell head over heels in love with Leahona Larson.

CHAPTER ELEVEN

HAWAII CALLS, AND I PICK UP

It came to pass on a sweltering hot day in mid-July, as I was sunning myself on a patch of grass in the city park. Lying next to me on the grass was my pal Clark Monk. From across the street I heard a car door slam; I looked up to see a young woman with waist-length blond hair walking away from a red Hillman Minx. It was the first car I'd ever seen that wasn't either a Ford or a Chevrolet.

"Holy cow!" I exclaimed. "Who *is* that?"

"Leahona Larson," answered Clark. "Her family just moved into the ward. From Hawaii. You *like*?"

"Well, *yeah!*"

Not only had Leahona's family just moved into our ward, they'd moved into a house only a few doors up the street from mine. The first thing they did was rip up the wall-to-wall shag carpeting and lay down hemp flooring. Then they sawed the legs off the dining room table, lowering it to knee level. Down came the drapes; up went bamboo curtains. At night, tiki torches blazed in the yard. The air in my neighborhood became an exotic blend of scents: sagebrush and pinion, orchids and orange blossoms. And something else, I didn't know what, but I liked it.

One Tuesday evening, Leahona's family put together a luau in the ward recreation hall. Following a feast of tropical punch and cookies, we were told to kneel in a large circle on the hardwood floor. The lights went down and Leahona appeared, tapping her long tapered fingers on a gourd and swishing her muumuu-clad hips in rhythm to the beat. It was a hula dance, but not your stereotypical grassy gyration. No, Leahona's dance was slow and sensuous. Her ankle-length muumuu left much to the imagination, and I have a great imagination.

"You're supposed to keep your eyes on her *hands*," I heard someone say. But the only hands I could see were those of Clark Monk waving back and forth in front of my bulging eyeballs.

I wanted desperately to become better acquainted with this exotic island flower that had miraculously descended from paradise into coal country; however, having never asked a girl on a date before, I didn't know where to begin. Happily, Clark agreed to set things up, provided he could tag along for the ride. And, as luck would have it, the movie playing at the Carbondale Theater that weekend was the Rogers & Hammerstein musical *South Pacific*.

Thus began my first Hollywood-inspired romance, in which I played the role of Rosanno Brazzi to Leahona's Mitzi Gaynor. From that night forward, she and I were "an item." In school we exchanged knowing glances across crowded classrooms. We made hap hap happy talk at The Milky Way and performed together in an MIA road show that was loosely based on Michener's *Tales of The South Pacific*. Leahona, of course, was the star; my part involved wearing a loincloth and beating on a conga drum.

Then there were the church dances—what were known as Gold and Green Balls. These took place on the church's basketball court, but not until the MiaMaids, using rolls upon rolls of colored crepe paper, had transformed it into a grand ballroom. Still, no amount of decoration could fully conceal the basketball hoops overhead, nor the stripes painted on the hardwood floor.

The underlying sports motif was reinforced by the presence of referees—adult chaperones charged with making sure no illegal contact took place between sexes. There was even a seamstress on call in the event a girl should show up wearing an insufficiently modest frock. Of particular concern at that time was an emerging fashion known as the "strapless formal." Any young woman brazen enough to show up wearing one would be hustled to a back room and summarily retrofitted.

Leahona's "formal" consisted of multiple tiers of baby blue taffeta, buoyed outward by crinoline petticoats sufficient to bind the wounds of the entire Confederate Army. The bottom tier measured ten feet in diameter, ensuring that the two of us wouldn't be dancing cheek-to-cheek. It was her mother's design.

A major problem: How to transport Leahona from her home to the dance? Luckily, every young lady's wardrobe in those days included an outer garment known as a car coat, into which she and her voluminous frock could be packed. Once inside the dance hall, all a boy had to do was unbutton the coat, yank on the belt and *poof*! His date deployed like a parachute.

The music was live, but only barely. Volmer Holm's venerable five-piece combo had played for countless Gold and Green Balls dating back to the 1930s. Though Holm remained surprisingly youthful in appearance, his tempo had begun to drag somewhat. We boys didn't swing our partners, but rather cautiously steered them in a counterclockwise direction round and round the dance floor—always under the watchful gaze of our adult chaperones. In effect, the affair was a lot like the Indianapolis 500 run under a yellow flag.

Once across the finish line, we'd repack our dates into their respective car coats and repair to Bishop Snarr's house for a non-alcoholic nightcap. Sister Snarr served root beer and cream-filled éclairs; the girls exchanged gossip while we boys took turns at the Ping-Pong table. It was a safe house—much safer than a roadhouse, where one could only get drunk, then perish in the obligatory car crash. The possibility we might end up *bored* to death was of no great concern, because Mormons are nothing if not gluttons for boredom. Nonetheless, I was reluctant to see the so-called party end, because then it would be time to bid Leahona goodnight, and I was dreading the moment. I dreaded it because I knew she'd be expecting a goodnight kiss. I had never kissed a girl, and the fact weighed upon my soul like an anvil. How should I go about it? Do I tilt my head? Part my lips? Close my eyes? Should I make like Rosanno Brazzi and burst into song?

All I knew about kissing was what I'd seen in movies. I'd also heard that a young couple's first kiss was supposed to take place on the girl's front porch, but not on the first date. Perhaps not even the second, but almost certainly the third.

This being our fourteenth date, I was worried sick how it was going to end. Not like the others, I hoped, with me hemming and hawing and staring disconsolately at my clay feet. No, this time I would take her hands firmly in mine and say something like, "Thanks for a lovely evening."

No—wait. "Thanks for a lovely evening," would be Leahona's line. Whereupon I will answer, "The pleasure was all mine."

No—wait. "Thank *you* for a lovely evening," I'll say. "And by the way, did anyone ever tell you that moonlight becomes you and that you have the loveliest eyes?"

No—wait! "Would you mind *closing* your eyes?" Then I would kiss her—but where? On the lips or on the cheek?

The more I thought about it, the more I began to sweat, until by the time we arrived at Leahona's house, my foolish heart was beating like a trip hammer. Her front porch loomed stark and foreboding as a gallows. Thirteen steps to the brightly-lit landing, where Leahona turned to face me, her car coat bulging as if to burst at any second. Tenderly, she took my hand in hers.

"Thank you for a lovely evening," she said.

"Yes, it was. It definitely was—lovely. Enchanting, in fact. It was some *enchanted* evening."

"Well—goodnight, then...." I heard the door open and close and in a rustle of petticoats she was gone. From far away a train whistle sounded, and for a brief moment I felt the earth move under my feet. Another coal train was pulling out of Carbon County.

CHAPTER TWELVE

REDEEMING THE DEAD, TRANSPORTING THE UNDEAD

That romance can blossom in a hick coal town in the middle of nowhere, just the same as on a tropical island paradise, is one of life's sweet mysteries. I'm glad I came of age at a time when romance figured larger than biology, before Masters and Johnson displaced Rogers and Hammerstein. Compared to an out-of-wedlock pregnancy or a sexually transmitted disease, virginity was an affliction I could live with—barely. I figured eventually things would change for the better—if not in this life, then in the sweet hereafter, where sexual relations with multiple partners in perpetuity awaits every worthy Mormon male. Andrew Marvell, eat your heart out! Even a shy, awkward, introverted adolescent like me could become an accomplished lover—same as a retired corporate executive could become a living prophet.

Indeed, even the deceased Catholic saint and the Jewish martyr will be redeemed—along with all those whose misfortune it was to be born before the true gospel of Jesus Christ was revealed to Joseph Smith. In the fullness of time, all will be afforded the opportunity to convert to Mormonism—thanks to posthumous baptism by proxy, better known as "baptism for the dead."

Here's how it works. Let's say that you were born in a mud hut in Afghanistan. Chances are, because your parents are Muslim, you will be taught to pray to Allah while facing Mecca—not Utah. Because there are no Mormon missionaries in Afghanistan, you will not hear about Joseph Smith and his miraculous vision; that is, not until after you pass on. Then, for the first time, you'll discover that heaven is a layer cake and you are in the bottom layer. You'll curse yourself for not having the good sense to have been born in Utah!

Happily, all is not lost. You'll have a second chance at redemption, provided you forsake Islam and embrace Mormonism. However, there is just one small complication. Although spiritual beings are able to engage in most of the same activities corporal beings do—making love and waging war, for instance—they *may not* be immersed in water. Thus, the only way for you to become a Mormon in the hereafter is to be baptized by proxy.

Another condition: Mortal Mormons can't perform this vital service for you until your papers are in order. The church *must* know your name—including your middle initial—the date on which you were born and the date that you died. Whether in fact you wish to join the one true church is entirely up to you; you are free to remain in spirit prison forever if that is what you desire. However, because you are dead, there is *absolutely nothing you can do* to prevent the Mormons from baptizing you by proxy. Rest in peace but rest assured that at this very moment some silver-haired sister is poring over microfilm in search of your name and vital statistics. And once she finds them, your information will be forwarded to the nearest LDS temple for immediate processing. Once a sufficient number of names have been "extracted," live bodies must be rounded up for the baptismal ceremony. Which is how, one fine day, I found myself a passenger in Bishop Snarr's latest car, bound for the Manti Temple.

What I knew about those ten souls on whose behalf I was about to be dunked was absolutely nothing. The main thing was that for the first time in my life, I was about to set foot inside the holy temple, an edifice that is off-limits to all but the worthiest of church members. These include ordained elders about to embark on missions, virginal couples intent on betrothal, married couples previously joined in civil ceremony who have subsequently decided to "solemnize" their union and have their offspring "sealed" to them for "time and all eternity." And, lastly, carloads of clueless teenagers out to have a good time.

Upon arriving in Manti, my priesthood pals and I were hustled into an anteroom by a white-haired gentleman attired all in white. In a soft voice he advised us of the house rules: No loud talking, no laughing, no gum chewing, and no towel-snapping—no horseplay of any kind. Then each of us was asked to present a document attesting to our worthiness, a slip of paper known as a temple recommend.

"Remember," said the white-haired gentleman. "You are in the House of the Lord, and you will be expected to act accordingly."

With that, we were ushered through still another door and down a narrow corridor to a dressing room that was unlike any dressing room I'd ever seen. There were no wet towels on the floor; the walls were unmarred by graffiti, and the tile floor was white and delightsome beyond belief. Silently, reverently, we changed into clean white shirts and trousers; then it was off to the baptismal font—and what a font! Not just an oversized sunken bathtub like the one in our ward house, but an ornately engraved bowl, balanced on the backs of twelve bronze oxen.

The temple font was large enough to accommodate the lot of us; however, custom dictated that we go under one at a time. As each boy surfaced, he climbed out and went to the end of the line to await another dunking.

Each baptism was preceded by a brief prayer similar to the one I'd heard recited at my own baptism. However, each time around, the elder doing the baptizing called out a different name.

"Ralph Waldo Emerson," I heard him say, whereupon my friend Clark Monk went under.

"Edgar Allen Poe." *Splash!* went Sven Jensen.

"James Fenimore Cooper." *Kerplunk!* went Barney Brown.

Gosh, I wondered. *Where did they dig up all these peculiar names?*

Now the elder had me in his grip.

"Brother Menzies, having authority, I baptize you, for and in behalf of Samuel Langhorne Clemens, who is dead, in the name of the Father, and of the Son, and of the Holy Ghost, amen."

Then the elder proceeded to push me under, but for some reason I was putting up a lot of resistance, thrashing and splashing like a Mississippi sternwheeler. *Who was this Samuel Clemens, I wondered? I sure hope he appreciates what I'm going through for him. Gasp!*

By late afternoon we had redeemed almost half a library card catalog's worth of nineteenth century American writers; now it was time to towel off and transform ourselves back into twentieth century teenagers. Soon we were homeward bound, Orrin Snarr at the wheel of his big new Chrysler Imperial, a car he'd owned for only a month—which for him was a long time. Normally, Snarr never kept a car longer than two weeks before trading it in on a different one. Vehicular polygamy, it was the bishop's only admitted weakness.

Bishop Snarr drove fast and none too carefully, considering that the lives of five young people were in his hands. However, he never worried about having an accident; we were, after all, Latter-day Saints on official church business, and surely the Three Nephites would see to it that no harm befell us.

The Three Nephites. They were my favorite flannel board characters, this trio of relics from ancient America who, having been given the option, had chosen not to die and go to heaven but to remain on earth indefinitely. The moral of the story is that immortality has its drawbacks. How hard it must be to outlive one's own time! To bury one loved one after another, to stand helplessly by, Dorian Gray-like, as one's lovely young mate gradually turns into a wrinkled old crone. Would you even bother to stick around, or would you be forever on the prowl for fresh young meat?

Nephite sightings occur regularly along rural Utah roads, where most often they appear in the guise of hitchhikers. Often as not, they are spotted by Mormons who are either going to or returning from the Manti Temple. In one oft-told tale, the driver stops on US 89 to pick up three bearded geezers. Moments later, as they barrel through Mount Pleasant at eighty miles per hour, one of the geezers speaks up.

"If I were you, brother, I wouldn't speed through Mount Pleasant. There just might be a child in the crosswalk."

Heeding the stranger's warning, the driver eases his foot off the gas pedal. Seconds later they come upon a crosswalk—and lo and behold! There *is* a child in the middle of the street!

Having narrowly averted disaster, the grateful driver turns to thank his passenger for the timely warning. Lo and behold! The backseat is *empty*!

In another story, one of the immortal Nephites appears in the headlights of a car filled with young Mormons on their way home from a fishing trip in the High Uintas. The boys stop to pick him up, then resume tearing down the highway at breakneck speed until the hitchhiker speaks up.

"Whoa!" he exclaims. "Slow down! There might be a cow in the road—perhaps just around this next corner, in fact."

The driver slows down, and sure enough, a cow appears in the headlights. *Whew*!

Five thoughtful minutes pass; then the driver spots what looks to be a young woman dressed in a tattered wedding gown, clutching to her breast a wilted bouquet. He recognizes her as the unquiet spirit of a jilted bride who, according to local folklore, roams the countryside in search of the lover who mysteriously disappeared a hundred years earlier. The startled passengers scream in unison; the driver's right foot moves toward the brake pedal.

"Oh, don't bother to stop," sayeth the Nephite. "She's a ghost. You can drive right through her."

CHAPTER THIRTEEN

WHITHER THOU GOEST, MIMSY FARMER, I SHALL FOLLOW

For me, the transition from high school to college wasn't so much a leap as it was a baby step. It so happened the nearest (and cheapest) institution of higher learning, Carbon Junior College, was only two blocks from the house where I'd grown up. By enrolling at Carbon and continuing to live at home, I could save a lot of money—and in our family, saving money was the most important thing.

Most of my chums were also staying put, the expectation being that they would attend junior college for one or two years and then be called to serve a church mission. Upon returning, they would get married, settle down, have children, and eventually start thinking about what they wanted to do with their lives. A surprising number would follow Orrin Snarr's lead and become optometrists.

So what were *my* plans for the future? The question was posed often in those days, and no one posed it more frequently than did Bishop Snarr. Once, he'd even made a house call, evidently concerned that I might be wavering from the career path he'd laid out for me.

"I'm not sure what I want to be when I grow up," I confessed. "Maybe I'll be a teacher."

"Oh, you're much too smart for that," countered Snarr. "I suggest you consider going into optometry. You can make as much money as a dentist, and you won't have to stick your fingers in anybody's mouth."

The fact my father, a schoolteacher, was sitting in the room didn't seem to faze the bishop, and why Dad didn't immediately show Orrin the door remains a mystery to me. If he had, perhaps we'd have been booted out of the church, and I'd have been spared a whole lot of trouble down the road. But no, my father seemed resigned to the notion that school teaching is a less than glorified profession. It doesn't bring in a lot of money, and as a result, schoolteachers never are appointed to high leadership positions in the church. Bishop, possibly. Stake president, rarely. General Authority? *Never!* Fact is, my father was fated never to rise above the rank of usher.

Happily, it wasn't necessary for me to make a firm occupational commitment right away, for at Carbon College, every course in the catalog was pre-something or other. My classmates were mostly neighbors and high school chums, and mostly all we talked about was our cars, the cars that belonged to other teenagers, and cars we would like to have but couldn't afford. Mine was a 1950 Mercury in which I could be seen cruising up and down Main Street, twin tail pipes burbling low, my left arm hanging out the window and pressed hard against the door in order to simulate a biceps. If I saw someone I knew, I would honk the horn, whereupon the honkee would honk back. That's how we were in the summer of 1961: young geese in a holding pattern, unsure of which way to turn. Most of us had a vague yearning to leave the nest—but how? Where? It is at this precise point that the Mormon Church begins issuing mission calls. And it was at this point that bishop Snarr became obsessed with my future plans.

Weekday afternoons I worked at a local garage as an automobile detailer. On weekends I'd drive my Merc five miles east of town to the county airport, where I had a second job as caretaker. The job paid only one dollar an hour, half of which went into flying lessons—but I liked it because I was on my own most of the time, which meant ample opportunity for creative daydreaming.

Come Sunday morning in a ward house five miles away, my name would be called—only this time there was no response. Such silence wasn't golden, and in fact was a matter of great concern to Orrin Snarr, who now began to fear that the erstwhile leader of the quorum had begun to stray.

"Looks like we're going to have to start holding priesthood meetings at the airport" he announced one day as I stood contemplating the underside of a 1959 Chevy Biscayne he had purchased the previous week. Snarr had brought the car into the shop to have it undercoated—a messy procedure that involved raising the car on a lift, then spraying hot tar under pressure inside the wheel wells and into every nook and cranny—including my eyes, ears, and nostrils.

"DON'T YOU THINK IT'S HIGH TIME YOU STARTED THINKING ABOUT YOUR *FUTURE*?"

Snarr was forced to shout in order to be heard over the roar of the air compressor. "SOON YOU'RE GOING TO BE NINETEEN YEARS OLD. DO YOU KNOW WHAT THAT *MEANS*?"

Of *course* I knew! Every Mormon boy knows what it means to turn nineteen.

"I THINK IT'S TIME YOU STARTED GIVING IT SOME *SERIOUS* THOUGHT," Snarr continued. "SURELY YOU DON'T INTEND TO BE DOING *THIS* FOR THE REST OF YOUR LIFE."

By *this*, was Orrin Snarr suggesting that were I to ignore his advice I'd be spending the rest of my life squirting hot tar onto the underbellies of Chevrolet Biscaynes? As a matter of fact, I *did* have other plans.

"I'M TRYING TO SAVE UP MONEY FOR COL-LEGE!" I shouted back.

"FINE AND DANDY!" Snarr replied. "BUT YOU MUSTN'T NEGLECT YOUR *SPIRITUAL* SIDE. MAN DOESN'T LIVE BY BREAD ALONE, YOU KNOW."

On that point the two of us were in agreement—except when it came to defining the word *spiritual*. To Bishop Snarr's way of thinking, *spiritual* applies to those precious few moments in a man's life when he's focused on something other than making money. Such moments occur only on Sundays, when he is sitting in church dressed in a dark suit, white shirt and necktie. But a person like me who spends his Sundays at the county airport, lying on his back on the tarmac, watching passing clouds—what is *spiritual* about that? An idle mind is the devil's playpen!

Orrin Snarr knew exactly how I should go about getting spiritual. First, I needed to let him know that I was ready and willing to serve a mission should God decide to call on me. Soon thereafter the call *would* come, and very soon I'd be on an airplane bound for some exotic part of the globe—which, in fact, was one of only two parts of the proposition that appealed to me.

The other appealing part: I would be treated to a royal send-off, or what is known throughout Mormondom as the "missionary farewell." Imagine an entire church meeting devoted entirely to you and you alone! Picture the bishop, his counselors, your family, the choir, the congregation—all singing your praises! Imagine a lovely young woman seated in the front pew, weeping and wailing and gnashing her teeth *because you are going away!* Imagine that you could be present at your own funeral—that's pretty much how I pictured my missionary farewell.

I *wanted* one in the worst way. I *wanted* to be the center of attention, to feel the love and approval of my community warmly washing over me. I *wanted* to have my picture posted in the ward display case alongside those of Joseph Smith and Jesus Christ and David O. McKay. For two and one-half years I would be our ward's ambassador abroad, their soldier in the field, their knight errant in shining armor! And when I returned, triumphant, I'd be hailed as a conquering hero. At my homecoming, I'd dazzle the membership with my command of Swahili. I'd captivate them with a tale of how Lucifer had done his level best to tempt me, and of how I had valiantly fought back. As for the French nymphomaniac who had chained me to a bed and ripped asunder my holy garments—I might just not mention that.

My sermon finished, I'd descend from the pulpit in a column of light brighter than the noonday sun into the welcoming arms of that special sister who had been saving all her loving just for me and me alone—for *two and one-half long years!*

On the other hand, there were some things about missionary work that did not appeal. For instance, missionary work. It had always been an ordeal to spend even two and one-half hours once a month home teaching; how could I possibly endure peddling the gospel door to door for two and one-half years? Moreover, I'd be making those rounds dressed as a teenaged Rotarian, in the constant company of another teenaged Rotarian. Not for one single minute would I be permitted to be by myself! There'd be no time for introspection or creative daydreaming. There would be no aimless wandering—only purposeful proselytizing.

Serving a mission would be like a church meeting without end. Nine hundred and twelve consecutive Sundays. How could I possibly stand it? Yet every which way I turned, I saw smiling faces urging me to go. Some were even offering to pay my way!

Fortunately, I still had some time before I'd have to make a decision. I was living in the pre-mission mode, a time when many young Mormon males seize the opportunity to live it up, knowing full well that their days of wine and roses are numbered. Thus it came to pass, in the suns-plashed summer of 1962, a group of my priesthood pals set out for West Yellowstone, Montana.

In those days Mormon boys and girls were much in demand at summer resorts, filling menial jobs that nowadays go to migrant Mexicans. Wages were low and living conditions mean; however, the fringe benefits were many. Rumors abounded of plentiful beer, cigarettes, loose women and general debauchery taking place in forested glades teeming with horned and hoofed creatures, with *geysers* spouting skyward at regular intervals in the shadow of the *Grand Tetons*. Truly, Western Wyoming was the geologic embodiment of our wildest wet dreams!

Because I was, after all, the most righteous of the group, I resisted the temptation. However, as the summer worn on, I grew restive; then came the phone call from Sven Jensen. The party was in full swing, he said, and a dishwasher position had just opened up at the Naughty Pine Café. He'd already spoken with the manager, who said I could start work immediately. Pay was only seven dollars a shift, but the waitresses were really friendly.

The following day found me behind the wheel of my 1950 Mercury, tracking due north through a series of lookalike southern Idaho farming communities. By and by, potato fields gave way to forests of lodgepole pines, split level ranch houses to log cabins. Then at last the basketball hoops affixed above barn doors became antlers. I had crossed into Wyoming.

Based on what I'd heard from Sven, I expected West Yellowstone to be like Las Vegas, except with bears. But it was nothing like Las Vegas. The business district consisted largely of gas stations and saloons, interspersed with motels, restaurants and souvenir shops, including the one where Rupert Ames was working as a cashier. When I walked in, I was startled at the sight of a cigarette dangling from his mouth. Rupert appeared startled as well, and quickly stubbed out his smoke.

"Brother Richard!" he exclaimed. "So glad you could make it. Listen, I'm on duty here until five. Why don't you just take my house key and make yourself at home?" I sensed he couldn't wait for me to leave so that he could exhale.

Down the road I located the tiny rental cottage where Rupert, Sven, Barney Brown and evidently a family of grizzlies had been spending the summer—and, like Goldilocks, I was disappointed at what I found: broken furniture, soiled laundry, dirty dishes, butt-filled ashtrays and empty beer cans. On the kitchenette table lay a dog-eared issue of Playboy Magazine, opened wide to reveal the August centerfold.

I was desperately searching for a clearing large enough to accommodate my sleeping bag when Sven came through the door, an open bottle of Coors in his hand. Quickly, he slipped it into his back pocket.

"Richard," he gasped. "How nice to ... *urp* ... see you."

The deal was this: For as long as Barney Brown remained in the county jail, I could have his spot on the floor behind the sofa. But I wouldn't need it until three o'clock the following morning, which is when my shift as dishwasher at the Naughty Pine Café would be ending.

Presently I found myself wearing an apron, up to my elbows in soapsuds. Being new to the job, I didn't realize I was supposed to periodically change the dishwater, which by ten o'clock that evening had turned the color and consistency of mushroom gravy. My only contact with the dining room was an attractive young waitress from Sheridan by the name of Shawn. Each time Shawn dropped off a fresh load of dirty dishes, she smiled—a *knowing* smile that seemed to say, "What's a nice Mormon virgin like you doing in a place like this?" As the night wore on, I began to ask myself the same question.

Shawn was friendly, but nowhere near as friendly as Floyd the Fry Cook. Floyd had been keeping a hungry eye on my rear end all evening, and after he learned I had no place to sleep but on a hardwood floor, he suggested I bunk up with him instead.

"Plenty of room in my trailer," he said. "And I've got some magazines you might be interested in looking at."

Contrary to everything I'd been taught in Sunday School, temptations such as those presented by the Naughty Pine menu were easy to resist. I wondered, *Is this the best the devil can do?* Shawn and Floyd both frightened me. Cigarettes and booze? I had no desire to befoul the holy temple that was my body. Perhaps I was in fact the exemplary Mormon that Bishop Snarr insisted I was. It was all very confusing.

The following morning I announced I was going home, whereupon Rupert and Sven became visibly agitated. They hastened to explain that the cigarettes and booze had been part of an elaborate joke they'd decided to play on me in order to make me think they had turned into bad boys. "Please don't tell Bishop Snarr," they said.

I laughed—not at the joke, but at their naiveté. Did they honestly think I was on a spy mission?

On my way home I made a detour through Jackson Hole, where my classmate and frequent road show co-star Claudette Birkenstock had a summer job as a waitress. If not for the plastic nametag pinned to her uniform, I might not have recognized her! No cigarette dangled from her lips, but gone was the aura of innocence. In only two short months Claudette had

Virtue Is Its Own Punishment

gone from innocent Mia Maidenhood to hard-and-knowing Wyoming Womanhood.

What is it about the cowboy state? I wondered. The answer didn't come to me until the following year, when I went to see a film titled *Spencer's Mountain*. *Spencer's Mountain* was the big screen adaptation of an Earl Hamner memoir that would later inspire the long-running television series *The Waltons*. In the big screen version, Hamner's Appalachian molehill became 12,600-foot Mount Moran. Henry Fonda and Maureen O'Hara co-starred as the cash-poor but land-rich Spencers, James MacArthur as their son Clayboy.

Other cast members included Wally Cox, Whit Bissell and Donald Crisp—but forget about them. The *real* star of the film, in my opinion, was teenaged ingénue Mimsy Farmer in her first billed role. Miss Farmer's career has since faded, and she probably doesn't know that at one time she had a fan club in Carbondale, Utah. That fan club consisted of two people: me and Clark Monk, who happened to be sitting side by side in the darkened theater.

You know who she reminds me of?" Clark whispered in my ear.

"Who?"

"Virginia Wilton."

A shiver shot through my loins. Virginia Wilton was the most beautiful girl I'd ever seen who wasn't a movie star. Like Mimsy Farmer's character in Spencer's Mountain, she was young, blond, rich, and from the big city. From Chicago, although her grandparents and a handful of country cousins resided in Carbondale. It was one of those cousins who had fixed me up with Virginia the previous Christmas when she was in town visiting her grandparents. I don't remember whether we went to a movie or bowling, but it must have been one or the other because those were the only two possibilities. Afterwards, I'd treated her to a scenic tour of the neighborhood in my freshly washed and waxed Mercury. From a bluff overlooking Wellington, I'd pointed with pride to the tallest building in the county—the Liberty Fuel Company's coal washing plant.

"I know about that plant," said Virginia. "My daddy designed it."

My heart sank. How could I ever hope to win the heart of a big city girl from Chicago whose father designs coal washing plants? What could a small town hick like me offer—other than my small town hick heart on a silver platter?

Since that evening I had pretty much given up on the project—that is, until that night at the movies when Clark Monk pointed out how much Virginia resembled Mimsy Farmer, who in spite of her elevated social status still falls for love with the disadvantaged Clayboy Spencer, with whom I felt I had a lot in common. True, we were country bumpkins, but *special* country bumpkins destined to make our marks in the wide world that lay beyond the sheltering hills. Moreover, Clay and I shared literary aspirations, and in those days I harbored a crazy notion that writing might somehow result in riches. Or at least getting laid.

Of course, Clayboy had gone a lot farther with Mimsy than I had with Virginia, from whom I hadn't heard a word since that unenchanted evening on a high and windy hill overlooking the Liberty Fuel Company coal washing plant. However, I was confident our paths would cross again. In Provo, where I had learned from her cousin she would be attending Brigham Young University.

So there you have it. After all these many years of lame excuses, evasion and lies, the *real* reason I decided to go to BYU. Because I was hoping to hook up with a young girl by the name of Virginia Wilton, who reminded me of the actress Mimsy Farmer, who had pretended to have a crush on James MacArthur in a movie that wasn't even a faithful adaption of a memoir written by Earl Hamner.

CHAPTER FOURTEEN

BISHOP SNARR TURNS UP THE HEAT

You? You went to BYU? Nowadays whenever anyone uncovers my dirty little academic secret, they gasp in disbelief. I take it as a compliment. It means, I *hope*, that I no longer bear the slightest resemblance to that pathetic little dweeb pictured in the 1964 Banyon Yearbook. It's amazing how much I look like everyone else on the page. To all outward appearances, I fit right in. I remember I was *trying* to fit in. I was trying because that's what I had been carefully taught, that conformity is the greatest virtue of all, and that blending in is a whole lot safer than sticking out. In addition to Miss Virginia Wilton, there was another motivating factor. The "Y" was a family tradition. Both of my two brothers as well as my father were alumni.

My brother Jim, to no one's surprise, had graduated with top honors. He'd mostly paid his own way with money earned as a teaching assistant in the chemistry department. Upon graduating, he'd married one of his students, a proper young woman from solid pioneer stock, in the temple for time and all eternity.

Chuck's sojourn at BYU had been somewhat less illustrious; indeed, there are lingering doubts as to whether he actually attended any classes. He lived far off campus, in an unapproved rental house, with roommates who were all natives of Carbondale. He never dated BYU coeds and attended only one sporting event—a basketball game at the George Albert Smith Fieldhouse from which he was escorted by security after throwing a punch at a returned missionary who had cut in front of him at the ticket window.

Most of what I knew about Brigham Young University I'd gleaned from leafing through my father's yearbooks. Under college president Franklin Harris, the church-owned college had enjoyed a reputation as a party school, and from the numerous mash notes inscribed on the pages of his 1933 Banyon, I surmised that my father, though somewhat shy, had turned a fair number of marcelled heads. A pretty blonde named Thelma had written, "I have heard lots about you and think you're nice. I hope I may get to know you better next year."

"We had lots of fun together," wrote Elizabeth. "Remember that night we went boat riding? Oh! Oh!"

Illustrations in the manner of Maxfield Parrish depicted Provo as Utah's Garden of Eden, where young couples strolled arm in arm in leafy glades, picnicked on the sunny shoreline of Utah Lake, scaled Mount Timpanogas, shot the rapids of the Provo River in inner tubes, took in talking movies at the Orpheum, shared a five-cent Susan Bar (the largest nut roll bar on the market) chased down by a cool, sparkling glass of Becker's Becco ("satisfying as beer"). In other words, *precisely* the sort of activities I envisioned for myself and Miss Virginia Wilton!

In other words, I was optimistic. I was hoping to distinguish myself academically and thus atone for not having been born the baby girl my mother had been wishing for, and for not becoming an Eagle Scout like my father. And for not becoming the Mormon missionary Orrin Snarr was still doing his best to turn me into.

By now it had become a regular routine. At least once a week the bishop would pull into the garage behind the wheel of his latest automobile.

"Richard," he'd announce. "I've been wondering. If you were to be offered a choice, would you prefer to be called to Arizona or, say, Maine?"

"Arizona, I suppose. But then, if it really were a matter of personal preference, which of course it isn't, then I think I'd prefer to be sent overseas."

Several days would pass. I'd be darning windsocks at the airport, and Bishop Snarr's new Cadillac Coupe DeVille would roll into the parking lot.

"Just for the sake of argument," he would begin, "let's say you *were* called to serve abroad. Would you prefer Australia or Europe?"

"That's a tough one. Australia would be my first choice; that is, provided I could wear shorts and an open collar. However, given the fact I'd be wearing a wool suit, I suppose Europe would be a better fit."

Two weeks later, I'd be sunning myself on a blanket on the tarmac, daydreaming of the Grand Tetons and Miss Virginia Wilton. An unfamiliar Lincoln town car pulls up; a familiar face appears.

"Richard, if you had your choice of European countries..."

"*France!*" I answered without hesitation. I'd been studying French at Carbon College, so already I knew a few simple phrases. Also, according to what I had gleaned from seminary, French girls are extraordinarily receptive to the gospel.

"So—are you saying that if God were to call you on a mission to France, you'd go?"

Tough question. I had to assume the bishop was speaking hypothetically, because as every Mormon knows, mission assignments are decided in heaven and are not subject to negotiation.

"Well, let's just say that I'd be sorely tempted," I replied. "However—as you must surely have heard by now—I'll be starting at BYU in the fall. I thought maybe I'd put in a semester or two, then decide whether a mission is right for me."

It wasn't a complete lie, for in fact I was beginning to weaken. Something my mother had told me in confidence was weighing heavily on my mind: that it was my father's unspoken desire that at least one of his sons would choose to go on a mission. I suspected it was Mom's secret wish as well, to one day stand up in testimony meeting and brag about her *own* Missionary-In-The-Field!

CHAPTER FIFTEEN

ONWARD STRIPLING WARRIORS

September came and I went—not to France, but to Provo. My parents didn't go with me, since Provo was only 75 miles up the road and I'd made the trip a thousand times before. Mom and Dad had grown up in Provo and my grandmother still lived there, along with a couple of aunts. So I could count on a home-cooked meal whenever I tired of cafeteria food. Over Soldier Summit and down Spanish Fork Canyon I drove, through the Red Narrows, a twisting corridor between steep canyon walls formed of conglomerate rock, past thickets of gambrel oak and dwarf maple trees. Then the canyon opened up and I caught my first whiff of Utah Valley: fermenting silage mingled with hydrogen sulfide gas. Since the time when my parents were young, the Utah Valley economy had shifted from agrarian to industrial. The orchards and berry fields of Orem had been replaced by a steel mill. In years to come the valley would undergo another paradigm shift, from steel to silicon. Then still another, from computer software design to multi-level marketing of various and sundry herbal remedies and miracle juices.

Just about everything that happens in Utah Valley nowadays can be linked to Brigham Young University—be it Marie Osmond's failed first marriage or Gary Gilmore's crime spree or the hijacking of United Airlines flight 855. That's because the "Y" isn't *merely* an institution of higher learning; in fact, it's not *even* an institution of higher learning. It *is* an experiment in social engineering, and the experiment's purpose is to determine the minimum number of individual rights permissible under the U.S. Constitution. But I digress. At the time I didn't know that. I just thought I was going away to college.

The year was 1963 and all incoming students were required to spend their first year of residency in a dormitory—a recently enacted rule I suspected might have something to do with my brother Chuck. I had been assigned to Allen Hall, an older dorm situated off campus in a leafy part of town that resembled the Provo depicted in my father's yearbook. Allen Hall was within easy walking distance of Academy Square, an aging compound of ivy-covered buildings where my father had earned his master's degree whilst plucking the heartstrings of Thelma and Elizabeth and Cora Irene. I was excited.

No sooner had I begun unpacking my bags than the resident dorm mother, who bore a faint resemblance to Deborah Kerr, pulled me aside. She had just received word that I'd been reassigned. To Stover Hall. Even though I'd only been a resident of Allen Hall for five minutes, I felt sad to be leaving. I was confused as well. Why was I being transferred? And where was this Stover Hall?

Turns out Stover was part of the so-called New Campus, one of several housing units comprising a complex known as Helaman Halls. Helaman is the name of a character in the Book of Mormon. Walter F. Stover, a native German and former president of the East German mission immediately following World War II, donated hundreds of mattresses and box spring sets to Helaman Halls, and I detected signs of East German influence in the architecture as well. There was no ivy climbing the cinderblock walls and minimal landscaping—about the same as one might encounter at a medium-security detention facility. The building stood three stories tall and my room, F-2109, would be on the middle level. But before I could move in I first had to check in at the front desk. There I was asked to raise my right hand and swear a pledge. The so-called "Oath of Helaman."

What? Who? I vaguely remembered having heard the name Helaman. He was one of those buffed-up *Book of Mormon* action figures, son of Alma and leader of an army of two thousand that had defeated an opposing army of dark-skinned Lamanites without having suffered a single casualty. The so-called Stripling Warriors. But the person administering the oath didn't much resemble a pre-Colombian warrior. His name, if I remember correctly, was Eldon Something.

Eldon's superior and high priestess of the tribe was a rotund, plain woman of a certain age who went by the title Sister Possum. I would later learn that Sister Possum had dispatched more young men to the mission field than any other head resident on the entire campus. In fact, sending young men on missions was *her* mission. On her office wall was a bulletin board on which were pinned hundreds of missionary "farewell" programs, each picturing a crew-cut, horn-rimmed, necktie-wearing Stripling Warrior.

Sister Possum eyed me in a way that led me to suspect she already knew quite a lot about me and wasn't particularly pleased with what she'd found out. Once I had stumbled through the oath, she ordered her lieutenant Eldon to show me to my room. On the way up the stairway, he filled me in on the house rules. "No girls, no loud music, no profanity, no pornography, no alcohol, no tobacco, no cola drinks. Abide by the rules and should you experience a spiritual crisis of any kind, feel free to consult with your resident assistant, Brother Sterling Golden. His room is at the end of the hallway next to the family room. Report to the family room at ten p.m. sharp for family prayer."

Family prayer?

My new home measured approximately eight feet wide by twelve feet deep. I had a desk, a chair, a bunk, a small closet and two drawers, one of which could be padlocked provided Brother Sterling Golden be given a duplicate key. This in case there was something in the drawer I wished to keep private until such time as someone in a position of authority decided it should be made public.

The next several hours were spent unpacking and trying to make myself comfortable. Then came a scratching at the door. It was Randy, my new roommate.

Whatever higher power dispatched Brother Rockwell to Paris must be the same that assigned this slack-jawed, jug-eared farm boy from Caldwell, Idaho to F-2109. Mr. Famous Potato Head! I struggled in vain to make conversation until darkness fell, at which time I just gave up and wandered outside. I made my way to the Cannon Center, a low-ceilinged bunkerlike structure that housed a cafeteria and a small lounge where one could allegedly lounge. On this evening the plastic chairs and Formica tables had been pushed aside and a record player brought in. A social "mixer" was in progress, but for some reason I didn't feel much like mixing. Instead, I prowled the perimeter of the ersatz dance floor, feeling very much unmixable. I scanned the room in hopes I might spot *you know who*. Lo and behold! There she *was*! Miss Virginia Wilton, smack dab in the middle of the crowd, gyrating in sync with some buff Nordic giant.

I jumped up and down, frantically waving both arms. "Virginia! It's *me!*" I cried. "Over *here*! It's me, *Richard*, from *Carbondale!*"

Virginia looked up; from across the crowded room her eyes met mine. She smiled and waved—not the same way I was waving, as if to warn Captain Smith that a collision with an iceberg was imminent—but rather like Queen Elizabeth greeting her subjects from the deck of the royal yacht *Brittania*. Then she went right on dancing with the Nordic giant.

Alone that night in my bunk, I lay contemplating the holes in the acoustical tile, trying as best I could to tune out Randy's snoring. How could I have been so naïve? Whatever had led me to think I could ever capture the heart of a beautiful rich girl from Chicago whose father designs coal washing plants? What a huge sugar beet must have fallen on my head! Perhaps I should have heeded Bishop Snarr's advice and accepted that mission call. By now I could be in France, where the girls, evidently, are not choosy.

Awash in self-pity, I drifted off to dreamland, which was a far, far better place than the world to which I awoke the following morning.

CHAPTER SIXTEEN

THE IMPORTANCE OF BEING LIKE ERNEST

The time had come to start thinking about what I wanted to do with my life. Two days remained before it would come time to register for fall classes; I spent them attending orientation assemblies and touring various departments. Aimless but hopeful, I wandered from one end of campus to the other in search of my future.

Because I'd enjoyed some success as a reporter for my high school newspaper, I decided to swing by the editorial offices of *The Daily Universe*. I was there for no more than five minutes before deciding against a career in journalism. How can I put it? A bustling hive of joyless enterprise. But at the time I couldn't say exactly what it was that put me off, because—let's face it—I was still in a larval stage and just as dull-looking as the pudgy, acne-afflicted girl who had risen from her desk and was now waddling in my direction. I knew I was dull-looking by the way her eyes lit up when she saw me. Welcome *home*, brother!

I beat a hasty retreat to the boxlike McKay Building, home of the Humanities Department, or at any rate what passes at BYU for a humanities department. There I declared myself an English major, which I presumed would be a good fit because I had always been a good speller. Only later did I discover that being an English major involves reading books!

Oh, well. I figured I could squeak by. After all, Bishop Snarr had often boasted of having coasted through BYU without ever once cracking a book—except for *The Book of Mormon,* of course. Snarr was of the opinion that reading too many books could be hazardous to one's spiritual health. Indeed, the public library was as dangerous a hangout as a honky-tonk roadhouse.

I'd learned my lesson the hard way. Asked to select a topic for group discussion at an upcoming fireside, I'd settled upon the theory of evolution. However, no sooner had I cracked open my library copy of Charles Darwin's *Origin of Species*, than Bishop Snarr sprang from his chair and slammed the book shut. Then, in front of all my friends, I was read the riot act. What was to have been a discussion of evolution turned out to be The Inquisition. Where had I gotten that book? *Why* had I brought it to the fireside? *What* was I *thinking*?

The episode had left me confused and in tears. It wasn't as if I was the first to bring up the word "evolution" in a religious context. In seminary class, Brother Rockwell had spoken disparagingly of Charles Darwin time and again. We had "discussed" Darwin's theory at length without ever once opening his book. We had not read one single word; all we knew about Charles Darwin was what we had heard from his detractors—detractors like Brother Rockwell who also had never opened the book. How is it that so many non-readers could be so opinionated?

"Because it's all a pack of *lies*," declaimed Brother Rockwell. "Man did *not* spring from a monkey! He was created by God, and in God's own image. God is *not* a monkey!"

Brother Rockwell went on to explain that God isn't a gaseous cloud or an elemental force in the universe, but rather a humanoid who bears a strong resemblance to the film actor Charlton Heston. Not *The Planet of the Apes* Heston, but *The Greatest Story Ever Told* Heston.

But what about those fossilized bones Professor Leakey had recently dug up in Africa? Homo Erectus with his beetled brow and prognathous jaw—was it not clear evidence that our early ancestors didn't exactly look like movie stars?

"There's a very simple explanation for that," explained Rockwell. "If you had a physical deformity, where would you have lived? In a *cave*, that's where. Where normal people wouldn't have to look at you every day."

A pretty convincing argument, I had to admit. But what about the dinosaurs? Turns out Utah isn't home to just the world's one true religion, but also some of the planet's oldest fossil beds. In the clay hills just south of Carbondale, paleontologists routinely unearth the petrified remains of gigantic prehistoric reptiles. If, indeed, the world is only six thousand years old, how did they get there?

"I'll tell you how they got there," thundered Brother Rockwell. "Brother Lucifer buried those old bones in the ground in order to challenge our testimonies!"

Brother Lucifer?

And now here I was, safe and sound at Brigham Young University, where my testimony wasn't likely to be challenged in any way. In order to minimize the risk of secular contamination, the administration had mandated that each and every student, regardless of his chosen field, take at least one religion class per semester. In subsequent years, in response to parental complaints that certain secular courses had become *too* secular, a second rule was enacted requiring that all instructors, regardless of academic discipline, be certified as temple-worthy Mormons. Years later came a third edict: No longer would it be enough that students be subjected to religious indoctrination during the week—nowadays, they are required to attend church on Sundays. So I suppose I should thank my lucky stars that I attended Brigham Young at a time when the atmosphere on campus was still relatively liberal—compared to, say, North Korea.

A *liberal* education, that's what I had in mind. The key would be to pick and choose my professors carefully. And by that, I mean professors who were on the cusp of being canned. Except for the obligatory religion class, I took care to steer clear of certain hotbeds of orthodoxy—such as the College of Business and the Wilkinson Student Union, so named in honor of Ernest L. Wilkinson.

The pugnacious Wilkinson was president of the university and also the school's mascot—Cosmo the Cougar. It was supposed to be a big secret just who it was inside the cougar costume, but I, for one, was never in doubt. I recognized the leonine posture, the predatory gait. In the Book Cliffs I'd once come within ten feet of a *real* mountain lion, and it hadn't scared me half as much as the time I came face to face with Ernest L. Wilkinson. It had happened on the morning of registration day, just inside the main entrance to the George Albert Smith Fieldhouse. There he stood, coiled and ready to pounce on each new student who walked in the door.

"Welcome to Brigham Young University," he growled, fixing me with a baleful gaze while firmly gripping my right hand in his right paw. In addition to the pain, I felt a chill coursing up and down my spine. I was terrified!

As a student in the early 1920s, Wilkinson had distinguished himself as school newspaper editor and star of the debate squad. He'd gone on to earn a law degree from George Washington and a doctorate from Harvard. In 1951 he'd taken over the reins of BYU and was presiding over an era of unprecedented growth and constant construction. Almost all the buildings on Upper Campus had gone up during his reign, including the soon-to-be completed Wilkinson Center. Dr. Wilkinson was proud of his many buildings, but even prouder of his success in politicizing the campus. In his memoirs, he would point out that when he took over, only 41 percent of the student body identified with the Republican Party. Within four years, that number had more than doubled to 84 percent.

By the time I came along in 1963, hardly anyone on campus was aware that a rival political party even existed. Certainly there was no diversity on display at the traditional welcoming assembly when Wilkinson rose to address a throng of freshmen and transfer students numbering six thousand strong. He spoke mostly of rules, reciting a long list of what would be expected of us, an even longer list enumerating a multitude of infractions that would result in immediate expulsion. At the conclusion of speech, he admonished all who were prepared to uphold school standards and *to help the administration enforce them* (italics his) to rise and shout.

According to Dr. Wilkinson's memoirs, during his twenty-year tenure only three students ever refused to rise and shout. "They were advised to go to the Treasurer and receive a refund of their tuition," wrote Wilkinson. "This commitment always set the tone for the rest of the school year and the students were off to a good start."

I rose, I shouted, and then slunk back to my little room at Stover Hall, where already I had become something of an enigma in spite of the fact I looked and dressed pretty much the same as everyone else. Try as I might, I was having trouble connecting. It was particularly difficult with upperclassmen, perhaps because they had all served missions. They continued the mission habit of traveling in pairs, like animals on the way to Noah's ark. They were somber and disinclined toward horseplay of any kind. Spontaneity was frowned upon, as were pranks, however harmless. I soon learned the best way to get along was to just keep my head down, which was especially important in the Cannon Center cafeteria, where my table mates never failed to say grace before digging in. I didn't know whether saying grace was mandatory or not, but why take a chance?

Although my dorm mates had come from all parts of the country, all were more or less the same. Each had undergone a similar upbringing. All were white and of northern European descent. I was the only one whose surname included the letter Z—a fact destined to become a genealogical stumbling block.

"What kind of name is *Menzies*?" they'd ask. "Doesn't sound Danish."

"It's Scottish," I'd answer. "You should know that; Scotland's not that far away from Denmark."

"But the Z—that's unusual, isn't it?"

"To *you*, maybe. Where I come from—Carbon County—it's a fairly common consonant."

Once my pedigree had been established, the interrogation would move to step two. Where had I gone on my mission? *"What?"* So, *when* was I planning to go?

After a few days, I gave up on direct eye contact. I discovered the best way to meet people at BYU was to employ my peripheral vision; that is, if I should catch a glimpse of someone slipping out the back way when it came time for family prayer, I would make it a point to track that person down and introduce myself. Which is how I became acquainted with an aspiring artist by the name of Dwight Weed.

Unhappily paired with a returned missionary roommate, Dwight lived just three doors down the hallway. He was runty with an olive drab complexion—the result of a longstanding addiction to nicotine. Like me, he had no idea how he had ended up at Stover Hall.

"I was hoping to live in an apartment," he explained. "But then at the last minute I got transferred. I feel like I'm a puppet in a play, and some puppet master offstage—I'm not sure who—is jerking me around."

Because his smoking habit consumed an average of two packs a day, Dwight spent almost all his waking hours off campus. An art major, he always took along his sketchpad and charcoals. Soon, I began tagging along. Our favorite getaway was Ironton, an abandoned smelter that lay just south of the Provo city limits. There we'd tramp the marshy industrial wasteland, kicking at pieces of junk and pitching stones into stagnant, sulfur-scented pools.

"It's funny," Dwight confided between urgent puffs. "I feel more at home here than I do on campus. Used to be, I'd go for a long walk every morning along Canyon Road—but then I noticed this strange car was following me."

"Kidnappers?"

"BYU Security, I imagine. You know, if they catch you smoking, even *off* campus, it's grounds for expulsion. And they have informants *everywhere*. I don't even know why I'm telling you this. For all I know, you could be one of them."

"I'm not a spy," I said. "Although once I was accused of being one—by some friends of mine who had gone to Wyoming for the summer to take up smoking."

"Would you care for one?" Dwight held out his pack of Salems.

"Uh, no thanks. Would you believe I've never smoked a cigarette in my entire life? Never touched alcohol, either. Gosh, I don't even know what coffee tastes like."

Dwight looked at me long and hard. "So where the fuck have you *been* all your life?"

"I dunno. In Church, I guess."

"Then you're no doubt familiar with what is called the Word of Wisdom?"

"Of course I am. It's the eleventh commandment: 'Thou Shalt abstain from tea, coffee, tobacco, liquor and cola drinks."

"Not *that* one, stupid," Dwight interrupted. "The Word of Wisdom says you better watch your *back*, brother! That's the gospel according to Dwight Weed. You can write it down if you like."

I *did* write it down—in a journal I'd begun keeping the day I moved into Stover Hall. Why, I'm not sure; I just had a premonition something big was about to happen—and happen it did. On page eleven of my diary, dated November 22, 1963, I wrote, "John F. Kennedy was shot and killed by a sniper in Dallas today. It doesn't seem real. Everyone is stunned."

At any rate, *I* was stunned. Stunned and depressed and unable to do much of anything that dark day but lie on my bunk and stare at the holes in the acoustical ceiling tiles. About mid-afternoon Mr. Famous Potatohead came crashing through the door.

"Did you hear the news?" he asked.

"Yes. And I'm really sick about it."

"Me, too. Who do you think is behind it? What do you think will happen if they shoot *our* president?"

"What are you talking about, Randy? President Kennedy *did* get shot."

"I know. But what'll we do if they shoot David O. McKay?"

I couldn't think of an adequate response. I was even more stunned and shocked than before, and I still couldn't move. Finally, Randy asked, "Why are you just lying there? Don't you have any classes this afternoon?"

"Classes?" The thought hadn't occurred to me. I had assumed all classes had been cancelled. But *no*—not at Brigham Young University! Not only had classes not been cancelled; even the evening's big social event was going ahead as planned. The so-called computer dance, it promised to match couples scientifically by means of information fed into a state-of-the-art IBM 1620 installed in the basement of the Smoot Administration Building. The room-sized device had been programmed to sift and compile information gleaned from individual questionnaires, then spit out a list of compatible couples.

In a moment of weakness, I had filled out one of those questionnaires.

A week later I had received in the mail a postcard bearing the name and telephone number of the coed who—according to the IBM 1620—was my one and only. To my infinite disappointment, it wasn't Miss Virginia Wilton from Chicago, but rather a freshman named Melonie, from a small town in downstate Idaho. Melonie lived in a highrise residence hall on the northeast corner of Upper Campus, on the bottom floor of which was a holding area reserved for gentlemen callers. In order to collect my date, I first had to state my business and present my student identification card to a stern-faced matron seated on the opposite side of a Plexiglas barrier. After examining the card, front and back, she pressed a button. Shortly thereafter a buzzer sounded, a door lock clicked open, and Melonie appeared. From the look on her face, I gathered she was no more impressed by the performance of the IBM 1620 than I was.

"Listen," I said, as I tamped her into her car coat. "If you don't feel like going out tonight, I understand. I mean, considering what's happened."

"Oh? What's happened?"

As we drove to the George Albert Smith Fieldhouse, I filled Melonie in on the grim details. A man by the name of Lee Harvey Oswald had fired a bullet into the back of JFK's skull as the president's motorcade passed by the Texas Book Depository in Dallas. President Kennedy had been pronounced dead on arrival at Parkland hospital; Lyndon Baines Johnson had been sworn in as the nation's new leader.

Long pause while Melanie gathered her thoughts. I could tell she was thinking because her eyebrows were knitted. Or perhaps she was born with knitted eyebrows, it was hard to say. I mean, she *was* from a small town in downstate Idaho.

"Do you like mountains?" she asked.

"*What?*"

"Mountains. I was wondering if you like them? On my questionnaire, I wrote down that I like mountains."

It took me only slightly longer than an IBM 1620 to process the data. One of the questions on the questionnaire had to do with where I would prefer to spend my summer vacation—at the beach or in the mountains? I must have checked the latter, only to regret it now.

"I just love mountains," Melonie continued. "I love singing and twirling on the tops of them. What about children? How many children would you like to have?"

"Oh, I dunno. How about six?"

"Bingo."

Our future plans laid, we proceeded to the George Albert Smith Fieldhouse, where we took our place in the bleachers alongside hundreds of scientifically matched couples. Looking around, I surmised that computerized matchmaking at BYU didn't involve a complicated algorithm, given the prevailing notion that it didn't really matter who one married, so long as one married a fellow Mormon. I mean, seriously, why even bother shopping around for a mate when we're all pretty much interchangeable?

As usual, the festivities began with an opening prayer, followed by a hymn. Then a singing group calling themselves the Tree D's—Mormondom's answer to the Kingston Trio—launched into a medley of folk songs, concluding with a stirring rendition of "When Johnny Comes Marching Home."

"In honor of what happened today," explained the D named Dwayne.

"A murmur swept through the crowd. "What happened today?"

The entertainment portion of the evening must have been followed by a dance; however, I don't recall dancing—with Melonie or anyone else. I don't even remember how my date with Melonie ended. The important thing was that it did eventually *end*, leaving me with a mistrust of computers that has persisted to this day—not to mention some lingering issues with mountains.

CHAPTER SEVENTEEN

DWIGHT WEED GOES MISSING

Dwight and I were spending more and more time together, ranging ever farther from campus in search of industrial wastelands littered with debris—raw material from which my artist friend would assemble *objets d'art* for his sculpture class. Now an abstract expressionist, Dwight had given up on realism after learning that BYU's art department offered no course in figure drawing. That is, no course in *nude* figure drawing. In the interest of modesty, "nude" models were obliged to pose in opaque leotards. Desperate to find out what a naked woman might actually look like, Dwight had turned to the fine arts section of the Ruben J. Clark Library. Alas, someone had razored out all the "racy" pictures.

Once, following a snowstorm, Dwight had sculpted a voluptuous snow woman, reclining seductively on the lawn beneath his window. No sooner had he finished than a mob of returned missionaries from the top floor rushed out and stomped her shapeless.

Watching from my window, I couldn't help remembering that poor, unfortunate porcupine. Not to mention the Fancher Party.

Years later, BYU would fall under criticism after the art museum's curator refused to uncrate Auguste Rodin's sculpture "The Kiss." Many were shocked by such prudery, but not this Son of Helaman. Censorship is the norm at Brigham Young, albeit in most instances it is carried out quietly, behind the scenes. For instance, Dwight once told me about a traveling exhibit of *avant garde* sculptures he'd help install. When his instructor discovered that one of the works was constructed of beer cans, it went straight back into the box.

"That's ridiculous," I said. "*Why?*"

"Because teachers here know better than to make waves," explained Dwight. "Make waves today, tomorrow you'll be out of a job."

In my own department, I soon discovered for myself the validity of the Gospel According to Dwight. Ever mindful of student spies, my instructors tended to sidestep any topic that might be deemed even remotely controversial. They took care never to assign reading materials that ran contrary to church teachings, or else they presented said materials in such a way as to suggest the author was either ill-informed or—better still—anti-Mormon! Once labeled anti-Mormon, any book could be dismissed as a pack of lies. Which meant we didn't have to read it, and most likely wouldn't be discussing it. When in doubt, leave it out!

The worst Ernest Wilkinson could do to a student was expel him, but he had the power to *fire* a teacher. And all an instructor had to do was let drop a single unorthodox remark that didn't sit well with an undercover informant, and the next day he'd be sweating bullets underneath a hot lamp in a small room in the basement of the Abraham O. Smoot Administration Building. Teachers who were summoned to the Smoot building tended never to return. Where they went, nobody knew. Rumor had it they were being shipped out of Provo in rail cars under cover of darkness to an undisclosed destination in the *East*—which is where so many liberal notions were thought to originate.

One morning I awoke with an original idea dancing in my head. I rushed down the hallway, intending to share it with Dwight, only to find that my artist friend had mysteriously disappeared.

"Disappeared? *When*?" I asked his roommate, who merely shrugged his shoulders.

"I dunno. He ducked out for a smoke yesterday morning and didn't come back. I'm guessing he probably got whacked."

More likely, Dwight had run afoul of the standards committee, which had the authority to expel any student caught smoking. Dwight's nicotine addiction had recently come to light following a spot contraband check—a regular feature of life as we knew it at Stover Hall. Senior resident Sterling Golden had a key to every lock on the floor, and if he found anything in your closet or drawers or underneath your mattress that didn't comport with school standards, you were in serious trouble. The only path to redemption was to tender a full confession, then fall to your knees and beg God and Brother Golden for forgiveness. I was pretty sure Dwight wasn't up to doing that.

Golden's bedroom/confession booth was situated at the far end of the hallway, next door to the family room. Golden wasn't just a returned missionary; he was the prototypical returned missionary. He was what Sister Possum might call a true Son of Helaman—or maybe even a Stripling Warrior. Except that instead of a breastplate for protection, he wore temple garments, also known as "magic Mormon underwear." Prior to embarking on a mission, an elder undergoes an endowment ceremony in the temple, after which his endowment is encased in a silken union suit that supposedly shields him from temptation and delivers him from evil. I, being the only unendowed upperclassman in the hall, was an anomaly. I was, as Brother Golden was wont to say, an elder who had tasted the milk, but not the meat.

Unlike me, Golden Sterling appeared to be thriving at BYU. Which is why I turned to him for help in a troubling matter, which—in retrospect—could have been swiftly remedied simply by transferring myself to an actual university. However, at the time I was still someone who—holy underwear or not—defined himself as Mormon. As such, I was trying my best to obey the rules and live up to the expectations of others. And yet for some reason conformity just wasn't working for me as well as it had in the past.

I was having trouble with a ward teaching assignment. It so happened my teaching companion was a recently returned missionary, as were most of the Budge Hall coeds we'd been assigned to "teach." Finding myself surrounded by returned missionaries, all of whom could recite whole pages from the *Book of Mormon* without falling asleep, was making me miserable. So one night I knocked on Brother Golden's door and begged to be released from my assignment.

"I think now would be a good time to ask Heavenly Father for guidance," he murmured. He directed me to kneel beside him on the linoleum floor.

"Dear Heavenly Father," he began. "We ask Thee to bestow upon Brother Richard the strength and fortitude to continue in his calling as an emissary of the Restored Gospel. Bless him that he might feel the holy spirit and be moved to continue in this important work, and bless the sisters of Budge Hall that they might likewise feel the spirit and be receptive to the monthly message, as revealed by the power of the Holy Ghost to the prophets, seers, and regulators of the Church of Jesus Christ of Latter-day Saints. Lift the scales from the eyes of this, your humble and obedient servant so that he might see more clearly the straight and narrow path that has been laid out for him. We ask this humbly in the name of Jesus Christ, amen."

"Do you feel it, Brother Richard?" he asked. "Did you feel a burning in your bosom?"

Sterling Golden was a man clearly more interested in receiving answers than asking questions—at any rate, he hadn't asked me any questions. Tears welled up in his eyes and his voice cracked as he gave me a pat on the shoulder and a firm Son of Helaman handshake. Whatever had been eating at me, he said, would eat at me no more. As long as I looked the part and continued to go through the prescribed motions, I would be just fine. *Everything* would be just fine.

CHAPTER EIGHTEEN

ENCOUNTERING AN ACTUAL EDUCATOR AND A HOT COED

Academically, if not spiritually, I was inching forward. My uncanny ability to spell long words and diagram sentences had made me Grammar Moses' pet pupil. Then there was Miss Kump, my composition instructor, who was instrumental in getting my first writing exercise published in the Wye Magazine.

The assignment was to compose a 2,000-word story adhering to the following plot line: "A conflict arises involving a religious figure who attempts to influence the thinking of a nonreligious character. The latter resists; tension builds toward a climax, which is followed by a resolution."

For once, I had the advantage of never having served in the mission field! So what I wrote was a variation of Edgar Allan Poe's "The Fall of the House of Usher" in which the ward recluse, Brother Roderick Usher, is paid a visit by his Mormon bishop, Percival

Merriweather, who is concerned about his boyhood friend's flagging church attendance—not to mention the run-down condition of the Usher residence, which is an embarrassment to the entire neighborhood. As the pair converse in an unkempt living room devoid of religious books and filled with unfamiliar objects, a commotion suddenly erupts from the cellar. Usher pretends not to notice it, even as the persistent thumping beneath the floorboards is joined by a cacophony of creaking hinges, splintering wood, and clanging chains. Merriweather's apprehension continues to mount until suddenly Roderick Usher's sister Madeline bursts into the room. Dressed in tattered bedclothes, her face mottled with red blotches, Lady Madeline is a frightful sight!

Denouement: It turns out that Lady Madeline isn't a victim of premature burial come back from the grave to exact revenge. No, she's been under quarantine because she has chicken pox—which is contagious. And the noise in the cellar?

"Lots of old houses have funny noises in the basement," I wrote. "Percival Merriweather never gave it another thought."

Miss Kump laughed out loud when she read the story—to the befuddlement of my classmates, none of whom had seen the humor in it. She gave me an A and offered to deliver the manuscript to the school's literary magazine editor, who agreed to publish it on Miss Kump's recommendation—even though he, too, saw no humor in it.

Delighted that I was about to see my first story in print, I set out in search of inspiration—which in Provo, Utah, isn't that easy to come by. So much of the bucolic landscape my parents had known had already been bulldozed away. Gone were the orchards and berry fields, the fragrant, verdant river bottom, the picturesque storefronts of Center Street. What remarkable buildings remained had fallen into disrepair and were mostly vacant, including the ivy-covered "Education Building" on Academy Square. A relic of the nineteenth century, the Education Building was where my father had gotten his college education, and it was where I was privileged to sit at the feet of BYU's oldest living faculty member: Gerrit de Jong Jr.

Professor de Jong had served as dean of the College of Fine Arts way back in the 1930s. By the time I came along, he was dean emeritus, and his teaching load had been reduced to a single class: Aesthetics 501. The class met at night, in a high-ceilinged, musty room behind a locked door that only Professor de Jong held the key to. There were just five students, including a Miss Garff and a Miss Graff, whom de Jong referred to as "the metamorphic twins."

We had no textbook and precious few assignments; basically, all we did was sit around and talk. Professor de Jong had assured us at the outset that we would all be getting A's, no matter what. "So please go ahead and close your notebooks, and let's open up our minds. Let's think about beauty, and beauty's metamorphic twin, which is truth."

Gerrit de Jong was a walking, talking history book. As a young boy growing up in Europe he'd sung in Mahler's choir. He spoke dozens of languages. He may or may not have studied painting under Rembrandt, but was conversant with chiaroscuro and the rule of thirds. He held up a print of *The Nightwatch*. Did we like it? Why? Why not?

"Don't be afraid," he assured us, casting a sideward glance toward the locked door. "We can speak freely here. These old walls don't have ears."

Some nights we'd assemble at de Jong's elegant Dutch colonial home on University Street. We'd listen to classical recordings, inspect his art collection, enjoy delicate pastries served upon imported Delftware. For one bright shining moment there was no blathering about Helaman and his oh-so-valiant stripling warriors!

Had Aesthetics 501 been the only course I took at BYU, I might look back upon my college days differently—*warmly*, same as my father looked back upon his. Alas, much had changed since the Thirties. The genteel era of which Professor de Jong was the last living remnant was gone, and very soon the study of aesthetics would also be a thing of the past. In universities across the nation, educators were being taken to task for failing to address contemporary, "relevant" issues. Old schools of thought were under siege and new questions were being raised, the answers to which—in the words of Bob Dylan—were "blowing in the wind." Before the decade was out, that wind would swell to hurricane force. But not at BYU, where all we felt was a gentle breeze. It came blowing in from the West Coast, from the sun-splashed beaches of Southern California.

The so-called surfer revolution didn't sit well with Ernest Wilkinson. No sooner had he stamped out East Coast liberalism, than along came West Coast hedonism. Brian Wilson and the Beach Boys led the charge, followed by a succession of beach-blanket-surfer movies based upon the novel notion that girls and boys just want to have fun. By the spring of 1964 the first skateboarders appeared on campus; I could see them riding imaginary waves on the sidewalks beneath my window. Did I join them? No! I was still too much of a Mormon to take a chance on anything different. I clung fast to the iron rod, never taking my eyes off the straight and narrow path that leads to what those in charge of the small, hermetically sealed world of Mormonism define as "joy."

In my journal I wrote that "sidewalk surfing" looked dangerous, and was no doubt a passing fad that would soon go the way of the upstart heavyweight boxing contender, Cassius Clay. Clay, I boldly predicted, wouldn't last even one round in his upcoming bout against the reigning champion Sonny Liston, who was a seven-to-one favorite.

On the very same page, I made note of "a bushy-haired English singing group from England calling themselves "The Beatles."

"Last week they came to the U.S., wooed all American girls between ages 13-18, and sold something like six million records," I wrote. "By the time anyone reads this, I'll wager that whenever anyone hears the word 'Beatles,' all that will spring to mind is little black bugs."

Nostradamus, eat your heart out!

Yea, verily, even as my brain continued to shrivel, I began to feel a stirring in my loins. It occurred to me that with the exception of Melonie from Idaho, I hadn't been on a single date. Perhaps it was time to stop brooding and start shopping around. After all, it was a girl who had lured me to BYU in the first place. Perhaps it was time to rejoin the hunt before all the good ones were taken.

Virginia Wilton was clearly out of my class; however, every day in the hallways I'd pass dozens of other Mimsy Farmer lookalikes. Some were walking arm-in-arm with guys who were even geekier in appearance than I. How *does* an ordinary-looking geeky guy go about snagging a hot girlfriend at BYU, I wondered?

The consensus among the Sons of Helaman at Stover Hall—the veritable mother lode of ordinary-looking geeky guys—was that there were two ways. One involved attending church services on Sundays; the other had to do with a social event known as a "cultural exchange." A distant relative of the frat rat-sorority chick hook-up, the cultural exchange was a closely monitored mixer wherein residents from an all-male housing unit would mingle with residents of an all-female housing unit. Libations being limited to nonalcoholic fruit punch and with not much in the way of hair on our heads to let down, such affairs had a tendency toward stiffness. Physical contact could be accomplished only by means of parlor games such as pass-the-lifesaver, the object of which was to transfer a lifesaver from a toothpick clamped between your lips to a toothpick clamped between the pursed lips of the girl standing in front of you. By pretending to be clumsy (no big stretch for a Son of Helaman), you might manage to steal a kiss—or, more likely, impale an eyeball. You might also become permanently cross-eyed, like the beefy coed who was fast closing in on me like a two-hundred-pound mosquito. Before she could strike, I ducked into the next room and dived behind a potted plant. It was there I came face to face with Scarlett, in whom all my hopes and dreams for future happiness would presently be invested.

Scarlett was a freshman from Minneapolis, where her father worked in upper level management at General Mills. She was an English major, had read my story in the school's literary magazine, and even remembered my byline! It was like a dream. I wondered, would literary achievement lead—as it had with Clayboy Spencer—to sexual fulfillment?

"Let's get away from here," she whispered in my ear. "The only thing dorkier than your friends is this stupid toothpick game."

"They're not *my* friends," I hastened to explain as I held open the passenger side door of my Mercury. "They are Sons of Helaman."

Smoothly as an otter, Scarlett scooted across the seat to my side of the Mercury. I heard the soft, seductive rustle of nylon brushing across Naugahyde and caught a strong whiff of Esteé Lauder perfume.

"Where would you like to go? The Creamery?" I asked.

Scarlett pursed her pretty lips. "Do you know where Rock Canyon is?"

I'd heard of it. Anyone who has ever attended BYU knows where Rock Canyon is—it's Provo's number one make-out spot. I'd been there once before, during the daytime with Dwight, in search of empty beer cans—which we found in abundance, along with half a dozen spent condoms.

In a leafy picnic area I found a space between two Volkswagen beetles and pulled in. Moments later we were locked in a passionate embrace. For the first time since moving to Provo, I was having a good time. All hardships to date were aught but speed bumps along the road to Promised Valley. And now at long last my travails were behind me and the celestial kingdom within my fevered grasp. But then I heard a still small voice crying, "Stop!" Was it my conscience? No, it was Scarlett.

"You *naughty* boy," she said, lowering her skirt and smoothing her petticoats. "You had better get me back to Tingley Hall right now. Bed count is at ten o'clock."

Technical virginity. Anyone who has ever dated a Mormon girl is familiar with the term. Basically, it means that one's date may be returned to her dormitory looking as if she's been run over by a McCormick reaper—so long as her hymen remains intact. No hymen means no temple marriage (technically speaking), which is why preserving the membrane is so vitally important. For Mormon males, technical virginity is harder to prove, although a painful medical condition known as "gold-and-green balls" is a fairly good indication.

The following Sunday, Scarlett invited me to Tingley Hall for a pot roast dinner, where we were joined by her two roommates and their boyfriends. Like me, the pair were squirming in their seats, evidently not fully recovered from gold-and-green balls. But there was no talk of that, no racy innuendo, no come hither glances, no footsie games played underneath the table. Scarlett acted so formal and proper; I was beginning to wonder if perhaps the Rock Canyon romp had been naught but another wet dream.

That same evening she dragged me to church, a place I hadn't been since moving to Provo. The proceedings—as I had feared—were a hundredfold more "spiritual" than anything I had ever experienced in Carbondale. The good part: Soon as church let out,

Scarlett suggested we pay another visit to Rock Canyon.

Thus was the pattern set: roast beef and mashed potatoes, followed by sacramental Wonder Bread crumbs and tap water, followed by a hot and heavy make-out session, followed by swollen testicles and guilt because we had come so precariously close to consummating the relationship. It got to the point I could hardly wait till Saturday, and could barely walk come Monday.

Occasionally on weekdays I'd get lucky as well. Scarlett would invite me to a book reading or insist that we attend an organ recital in the Joseph Smith Building. Or else she'd tell me to meet her in the J. Reuben Clark Library at such and such an hour—which is how I came to find out there was a library on campus. I was looking forward to playing hands-below-the-table; however, all Scarlett wanted to do was discuss the poetry of T. S. Eliot. The fact I hadn't heard of the man, let alone read his poetry, annoyed her to no end.

"Haven't you ever read *anything*?" she asked. "Where have you been all your life?"

One weekend, I offered to show her where I had been—hoping a visit to my humble boyhood home in Carbondale would cause Scarlett's heart to melt, same as Mimsy Farmer's heart had melted when she discovered that Clayboy Spencer's family lived in a rustic log cabin at the foot of the Grand Tetons. The so-called Big House? In Scarlett's view, it might as well have been a log cabin.

I was excited at the prospect of introducing Scarlett to my little corner of the world! Unfortunately, Scarlett didn't seem half as excited, and as we crested Soldier Summit and descended into Carbon Canyon, her face began to register signs of disappointment. Rounding Windy Point, we beheld the splendor of Carbondale's most imposing structure: the multi-storied, soot-covered ABC Coal Company tipple. Scarlett gasped, I assumed at the majesty of it.

We continued on, passing railroad switchyards, auto junkyards, dilapidated barns, the Motor-Vu Drive-In, the bowling alley. Scarlett pursed her pretty lips—transfixed, no doubt, by the variegated culturescape.

Hoping to make a favorable impression on her future daughter-in-law, my mother had scoured the house from top to bottom and hauled out the good dishes and silverware. As per custom, the Sunday meal consisted of pot roast and mashed potatoes, green beans and freshly baked bread. And—just as I knew she would—Scarlett charmed the pants off my parents. She was the *perfect* girl to take home to mother—neither too plain nor too glamorous, but just right. Best of all, she wasn't the least "put on" as Mom would later phrase it. No doubt about it, Scarlett was adept at making a first impression. Even I—who should have known better—was a bit bowled over.

"We just absolutely *adore* Scarlett," Mom wrote me afterward. "Your father and I agree you've done very well for yourself at BYU."

Because she had been brought up in a wretched little mining camp called Eureka, Mom was unfamiliar with the word "class." In particular, she was unaware of the Mormon class system—and until I landed in Provo, so was I. In spite of the fact there are no fraternities or sororities at Brigham Young, everyone just seems to know that some families are better than others. They know because the fathers are business executives, not day laborers. They know because their mothers, unlike mine, don't work as school lunch ladies. In fact, they don't work at all. They don't have to because there is always plenty of money rolling in. Their sons don't work as dishwashers and assistant janitors. Basically, all they have to do is go on missions, which makes them eligible to assume their rightful roles as mid-level business managers. No matter that they soon grow fat and their hair falls out, Mormon girls consider them a good catch. After all, they hold the priesthood.

"Your family is ... *nice,*" said Scarlett as we drove back to Provo. Followed by silence.

I tied to imagine what *her* family might be like. Her father being an executive at General Mills, I assumed he must wear a suit and tie just about all the time. Her mother? Probably not as good a cook and housekeeper as mine—but then, maybe she didn't have to be. Maybe they had servants, and instead of a dining room, a banquet hall. Most likely they didn't have sock fights after supper.

In the weeks that followed, Scarlett redoubled her efforts to remake me into someone she wouldn't be ashamed to take home to meet *her* parents. She began by compiling a lengthy reading list.

"Start at the bottom and work your way up," she ordered. "You should be able to get through them all during summer vacation, provided you don't waste all your time at the bowling alley."

I promised I would try. Anything to get back to Rock Canyon!

CHAPTER NINETEEN

DRIVEN TO DRINK BY A SCARLETT LETTER

Spring semester drew to a close. As my remaining days at Stover Hall dwindled to a precious few, I began to feel as if a great weight was being lifted from my shoulders. The black cloud that had hovered over campus lifted, revealing the huge block "Y" planted on Y Mountain. May 6 was designated "Y" Day, a school holiday during which a bucket brigade numbering in the thousands sets out with buckets of whitewash. I was watching the proceedings from my dorm window when Randy burst in, upset because his term paper had come back with a big red "E" scrawled on it. Evidently Randy's freshman composition instructor had accused him of plagiarism.

"It's much too well-written to be your work," he had declared.

Since I was the one who had ghostwritten Randy's paper, I took the criticism as a compliment. And, to be honest, it didn't exactly break my heart that Randy had failed the class. Better that plagiarists be pinched back early, before they go on to start religions.

Two days later, Mr. Famous Potato Head and I parted company, our paths never to cross again. I later learned Randy had been called to serve a mission that summer—news that didn't exactly surprise me. Sister Possum was delighted. Another missionary farewell program to add to her Warhol-like display.

With a sigh of resignation, Sister Possum accepted my room key and hung it on a peg-board alongside the others. I couldn't help noticing that all the room keys on the board—like all the faces on the wall—looked the same.

Soon I was back in my basement bedroom in Carbondale, reading about Thomas Wolfe's hometown in *Look Homeward, Angel* and knowing all too well what he meant when he titled a later book *You Can't Go Home Again.* Nothing had changed, yet nothing felt the same. Upstairs, I could hear the television set, but I had no desire to watch. Bedtime would roll around, but I wasn't sleepy. I'd slip out the back door and walk the darkened streets, past darkened houses. Where *was* everybody? Carbondale was like a graveyard with streetlamps.

I missed Scarlett terribly. As a parting gift, she'd given me a female mannequin leg encased in a black fishnet stocking. If it was her goal to drive me mad from unrequited lust, she was doing a fine job of it! How she was getting on in Minneapolis, I could only guess. Two weeks had passed and she had yet to respond to any of my impassioned letters. I had a bad feeling that she had moved on—something that simply wasn't possible for me in Carbondale, where all the girls I used to know were now pregnant by returned missionaries.

Meantime, in a basement bedroom one block away, my friend Clark Monk—home for the summer from the University of Utah—was suffering similar torments. The two of us would drive around town together, go bowling, take in a movie, suck down a milk shake at the Milky Way, where the median age of the clientele looked to be about fourteen. We had no contemporaries. We called ourselves The Two Nephites.

We avoided going to church, mainly because there was no place for us there, all the other young men in our age group having departed for the mission field. First to go had been Rupert Ames, better known to us as "Pip Squeak." We had attended Rupert's missionary farewell, where for a change no one had remarked upon his slight stature and lack of secondary sexual characteristics. On the contrary, he had been *lionized*! Rupert tearfully thanked his parents for having brought him up right; he thanked Bishop Snarr for helping to keep him on the straight and narrow path to righteousness. He even thanked Brother Rocky Rockwell for teaching him that just *thinking* about sex is bad. He didn't acknowledge "that special someone" in the congregation who had promised to wait for him, because there was no such person. But surely, upon his return, someone would show up to greet him at the airport. Otherwise, what was the point of serving a mission?

Next to be called was Sven Jensen, who went out—literally—with a bang. Shortly before his scheduled "worthiness" interview with the stake president, Sven had invited his priesthood pals to join him for a "repentance ceremony" in the foothills west of town.

There he set a six-pack of Coors beer on a rock; then we took turns firing away with Sven's .22-caliber rifle. After the last bottle had been shattered, Sven solemnly withdrew a pack of cigarettes from his shirt pocket and flung it into the sagebrush. Come time for next week's worthiness interview, Sven could truthfully answer that he kept the Word of Wisdom.

"From now on, it's *Elder* Jensen," he declaimed. "Look on my name tag, ye mighty, and despair!"

"You're completely full of crap, Sven," I said. "You can't even read the sacrament blessing off a cue card, let alone The *Book of Mormon*. My guess is, they're going to assign you to Salt Lake City. You'll spend the next two years going door to door in search of someone who isn't already a Mormon. Good luck with that!"

But I was wrong. When his mission call came, Sven had hit the jackpot. New Zealand! I was green with envy. Bishop Snarr had never mentioned New Zealand to *me*.

One after another, my old gang became pictures posted on the ward bulletin board, and with each departure the pressure on me to serve diminished. Orrin Snarr stopped coming around; I sensed he no longer viewed me as the leader of the pack. Hell, maybe I wasn't even a *member* of the pack! In some fundamental way I'd become a disenfranchised member of the community. Even my own mother seemed disappointed in how I'd turned out.

"When are you going to find a job?" she kept asking. "I hope you're not planning to sit in your room reading books all summer. Your father and I had to work when we were your age. Do you think money grows on trees?"

Virtue Is Its Own Punishment

Under the circumstances, I had no choice but to answer yes when Ivan Ames offered me a job at his tire shop. Ivan was Rupert Ames's stepfather, a brute of a man with hands like bear paws and a rapidly advancing hairline. For years Rupert had toiled in the tire shop as Ivan's unpaid assistant, and I strongly suspected it was a distaste for vulcanized rubber—not love of the gospel—that had propelled him into the mission field. And now that I had taken over his job, I took small comfort in knowing that Rupert had gone to a better place.

Ivan sold new tires, but the bulk of his trade involved retreading used ones—"castings," he called them. Ivan would splash on some glue, slap on a fresh layer of rubber, and pop the old tire into a molding machine. *Voila!* Out would come a facsimile of a new tire!

It took me all of an afternoon to master the skills by which Ivan had earned his living for over forty years. What I couldn't fully grasp was the mystery of how a man like Ivan can spend an entire lifetime minding a roadside tire shop in the middle of nowhere? Did he not have any higher aspirations? Anything to look forward to? I soon discovered that the two of us had something in common in that we were both daydreamers. I daydreamt about returning to Provo and the warm, waiting arms of my beloved Scarlett. Ivan daydreamt about the next life and the glory that awaited him in heaven—thanks to all the sacred code words and special handshakes he'd learned in the temple. Should a car fall off the lift or the air compressor explode, there'd be no waiting in line outside the gilded gates for Ivan Ames.

"Ivan!" a voice like that of Charlton Heston would boom out. "Welcome *home*, Ivan."

All heads would turn as Ivan stepped forward, proudly displaying his temple recommend before exchanging a novelty handshake with Saint Peter. Instead of dirt-caked, oil-stained overalls, Ivan would be clothed in exceedingly white temple garments. His skin would no longer be wrinkled and chapped, his bones no longer creaky. Like a retreaded tire, Ivan Ames would be almost as good as new.

Ding! A car would pull up to the pump out front and Ivan would come back to earth. But soon as the customer was on his way, Ivan's spirit would again take flight.

"It's a far, far better world than this one," he assured me. "Did you know that in heaven there is no such thing as a homely woman? Can you believe that? All the sisters in heaven are beautiful."

"Are the men beautiful as well?" I asked. "Or do they look like us?"

"Does it matter? As priesthood holders, we'll be in great demand. And busy—because as you know, one of our main duties after we leave this sphere will be to populate new planets."

I was familiar with the Mormon concept of sex after death. It was one of the arguments Scarlett had advanced against "going all the way" in the back seat of my Mercury. If only we could hold out, she said, we would remain eligible to be married in the temple, after which the two of us could engage in sexual intercourse not only for the rest of our mortal lives but throughout time and all eternity.

Ding! Dang, another customer! Fill up the tank, check the oil, wash the windscreen. The gulf between my real life and my daydreams grew wider by the hour.

I'd written Scarlett almost every other day, but as June wore into July, only one or two letters postmarked Minneapolis had appeared in my mailbox. Mostly she chatted merrily about her summer job as a sales clerk in an upscale women's apparel store. Surrounded by mannequins wearing fishnet stockings and lacy underwear. *Damn!*

"Tell me, how is your summer reading program going?" she continued. "What do you think of e. e. cummings? Please tell me you've gotten as far as the e's."

"Of course I've got to cummings," I wrote back. "I'm in the F's now. Capital F as in Flaubert. I just started on *Madame Bovary*."

But of course it was hard to stay focused on Flaubert, what with continual interruptions in the form of cars pulling into the station, tires baking in the oven, buzzers buzzing and bells ringing. Still, I pressed on, ever hopeful. And then came the letter I'd been secretly dreading.

"Dear Richard," it began. "I've been doing some serious thinking ..." and ended, "... hope that we can still be friends." In between the words "dear" and "friends" there was some stuff about how much Scarlett "respected" me—as if "respect" was what I most craved. As for remaining "friends"—well, I already had a friend in the person of Clark Monk, a friend whose love life was even more imaginary than mine.

The Scarlett Letter had arrived on a Thursday morning, and because Ivan was out of town doing temple work, I couldn't call in lovesick. So for the next several hours I had no shoulder to cry on, no one to tell my sad story to. Then, shortly before closing time, Clark Monk came by, wearing a face that was even longer than mine. His mother had just died.

The funeral took place in Clark's ward house, which was identical to mine except with a different congregation. The only person I recognized right off was Rocky Rockwell, who had served as Clark's home teaching companion and who thus presumed to know something about the Monk family, which—like mine—was only nominally religious. Nonetheless, Rocky had been pushing hard to bring Clark into line by sending him on a mission. Failing that, he'd assigned himself the solemn duty of "eulogizing" the late Mrs. Monk. As he stepped to the podium, those in the front pew reached for their raincoats and umbrellas.

"Nothing would have pleased Sister Monk more," he sniffled, "than to see her son sitting here today in his suit and necktie. Let us all hope and pray that Brother Clark will reconsider his plan to enlist in the military. Let us pray—sob—that he will resume attending church on a regular basis, and begin paying his tithing, in order to become worthy to serve as a missionary in *God's Army*."

The weekend following his mother's funeral, Clark suggested the two of us pack up the Mercury and flee into the desert for some mutual grieving. Thus it came to pass that—for the first time in my life—I tasted beer. How ironic, I thought, that the two of us had been driven to drink by a seminary teacher and a BYU coed!

"Here's to that hypocritical slut Scarlett!" I shouted—loud enough that the rabbits all around could hear.

Clark's bottle of Lucky Lager clinked against mine. "I'll drink to that. Here's to your lost love, your broken heart, your failure to amount to anything in the eyes of your community."

"Amen, brother. And here's to you, Clark Monk, who I predict will prove an even bigger disappointment. And speaking of disappointments, what is this I keep hearing about you joining the Army?"

"It's true. What else can I do? I'll be losing my draft deferment after I graduate from college. So I either go on to graduate school, go on a mission, or get married. I can't afford graduate school, I don't want to go on a mission, and it appears that no woman on earth will have me. So I can either wait to be drafted or enlist. If I enlist, I'll have more options."

Now that Scarlett had dumped me, my options were pretty much the same. But something about the military just didn't appeal to me. And it certainly wouldn't make me more attractive to Mormon girls, who tend to view men in military uniforms as spiritually substandard. Unlike missionaries, a Mormon boy who goes off to war isn't given a big send-off. And when he comes home—*if* he comes home—he's not hailed as a conquering hero. That is, unless he has managed to convert the enemy to Mormonism.

It wasn't the same thing as jumping off a cliff, but at the time it was close. What with America's deepening involvement in Vietnam, the probability of being killed in action was on the rise. Since grade school, Clark and I had been taught that every twenty years the Tree of Liberty must be watered by the blood of America's youth. Nearly two decades had passed since Hirohito had turned over his sword to General MacArthur, who in turn had handed it to Terry's father. So by now that so-called Tree of Liberty must be getting thirsty.

"But what about Korea?" I asked. "We lost over fifty thousand men over there. So don't you think that tree can hang on for a few years yet?"

"Korea wasn't a war," replied Clark, uncapping another bottle of Lucky Lager. "According to the history books, it was a 'police action' undertaken by the United Nations."

"So I've heard. But still, *fifty thousand* American soldiers dead ..."

"Which is why I intend to enlist instead of waiting to be drafted," Clark continued. "I don't intend to be cannon fodder; I'm going to be an officer. I want to be the guy who tells the others when it's their time to go in—not the other way around. How about you?"

"Well, I suppose I'll go back to BYU and try to hang onto my student deferment for a while yet. Brigham Young is hell, but at least they're not shooting at me."

"Not yet, they're not. Just give them time."

CHAPTER TWENTY

A LIGHT AT THE END OF THE FUNNEL?

September, 1964. All across America, change was afoot. President Lyndon Johnson had just signed into law the first broad-based civil rights bill, even as Georgia's Lester Maddox was urging his restaurant customers to wield ax handles against uppity black folk. At Berkeley, Mario Savio was about to launch the Free Speech Movement. In Vietnam, the United States had upped its troop commitment to 21,000. Long hair and miniskirts were the rage on campuses across the country—except at BYU, of course, where skirts were steadily getting longer and men's hair styles shorter. Indeed, the so-called winds of change were barely sufficient to ripple the American flag as it was ceremoniously raised each morning on a flagpole in front of the Smoot Administration Building. As the flag ascended, a recording of the national anthem blared from a multitude of loudspeakers, and no matter where you happened to be when the music sounded, you were expected to stop dead in your tracks, place your right hand over your heart, and face in the direction of the Smoot Building.

Throughout the entire tumultuous decade of the 1960s, there would be but one student demonstration at Brigham Young—staged by four placard-waving coeds in front of the school cafeteria. Their demand: larger portions of French fries.

I had settled into a small room just off campus, in the basement of Mary Mower's bungalow on Sixth North Street. My new roommate was Robbie Bruce, a business major from California. Recently returned from the Guatemalan mission field, Robbie wasn't like any other returned missionary I'd met. He didn't wear horn rim glasses, nor did he wear temple garments. On occasion, he would poke fun at the church—something not permitted at Helaman Halls. Robbie entertained doubts regarding the authenticity of *The Book of Mormon* and even questioned the divine right of the Republican Party to rule the Universe. In sum, he was as companionable a roommate as I could possibly ask for, given the circumstances.

By now I was determined to become a writer, although I hadn't told my parents, who, if they knew, would surely cut off my meager allowance. If my funds ran out, I'd be forced to drop out of college, and if I were to drop out of college, I'd be reclassified 1-A by my draft board. Before long I'd find myself in some rice paddy in Vietnam, plunging forward into the Valley of Death on the orders of Second Lieutenant Clark Monk.

I had decided the safest course would be to stick it out, no matter how much I hated BYU. By enrolling in as many "liberal" courses as possible, by skipping church and devotional assemblies, and by living off campus, I imagined I could pursue—insofar as it was possible in Utah County—a bohemian lifestyle.

I had acquired a small Honda motorbike, and when not in class I could be found at the leading edge of a dust contrail on the sage flats west of Utah Lake. On weekends I'd putter up Provo Canyon to Heber Valley, where I'd spread a blanket beside a mountain stream and sit down to a bohemian repast of Wonder bread and Velveeta cheese—the only brands of bread and cheese available locally. I'd read from the *Rubaiyat of Omar Khayyam*.

I enrolled in Dr. Clinton Larson's English 318: *Advanced Imaginative Writing*, which was a haven for campus misfits. Beside myself, there was Scott, a victim of muscular dystrophy who penned odes to whales and played sonatas on the piano with his knuckles. And Steve, who was BYU's first and only beatnik. A free-roaming radical from Southern California, Steve wore wraparound sunglasses and a goatee—in defiance of the grooming code. His *métier* was free verse; however, his primary function in class discussions was that of *agent provocateur*. There was Susan, whose snug-fitting black leotards aroused the trousers, especially those of Maynard, introverted author of *Cantos of Desolation and Despair*.

Maynard's uniform consisted of a black turtleneck sweater festooned with seminary pins and attendance medallions. It was unclear whether he was striving toward irony or undergoing a psychotic breakdown. He was the sort of person who, when spotted at a political rally, immediately drew the attention of the Secret Service.

One day Dr. Larson read aloud a selection from Maynard's cantos. The big problem, he announced, was the author's apparent ignorance of prosody. As a result, the poems read like nursery rhymes. To underscore his point, Larson *sang aloud* a poem Maynard had composed—which happened to deal with premature burial. At the conclusion of the "reading" Maynard shot out of his chair, snatched his manuscript from Dr. Larson's hands, and stormed out the door.

There followed a shocked silence. Those of us whose manuscripts were yet to be critiqued were especially shocked and silent. I had never heard the term "prosody" before. I made a mental note to look it up at the first opportunity.

How would I handle *literary* rejection, I wondered? Would it break my heart the same way Scarlett's letter had? Would it crush my spirit the way it had Maynard's? Would I be a failure in the eyes of my classmates, same as in the eyes of Orrin Snarr, Sterling Golden, Brother Rockwell, Sister Possum? Is there no end to the number of people I was destined to disappoint in this life?

To my surprise and infinite relief, Dr. Larson *liked* the short story I'd turned in. "A masterpiece of periphrasis," he called it. I made a second mental note, to look up the word *periphrasis*.

Thanks in no small part to Scarlett's Fishnet Stocking Summer Reading Incentive Program, I had become conversant with many of the standard works of English literature; that is, I knew the right names and allusions to drop in order to make a favorable impression in academic circles. I had read and reread *Strunk & White* as well as Mark Twain's assessment of

James Fenimore Cooper. I was beginning to see the difference between good writing and bad writing; to wit:

> I, Nephi, having been born of goodly parents, therefore I was taught somewhat in the learning of my father; and having seen many afflictions in the course of my days, nevertheless, having been highly favored of the Lord in all my days; yea, having had a great knowledge of the goodness and the mysteries of God, therefore I make a record of my proceedings in my days.

What Mormons call the "perfect book" Twain described as "chloroform in print."

And he was right! No wonder I had struggled so to stay awake in seminary class, snapping to attention only whenever Brother Rockwell put down the perfect book and resumed his ongoing reverie regarding the libidinous French girl. I was always told I would know the *Book of Mormon* is true when, after reading it, I felt "a burning in my bosom." But that never happened. In fact, I'd never been able to struggle through more than the first few pages before falling asleep. Conversely, a well-crafted paragraph from Thackery had the opposite effect:

> No more firing was heard at Brussels—the pursuit rolled miles away. Darkness came down on the field and city: and Amelia was praying for George, who was lying on his face, dead, with a bullet through his heart.

How was it that such a grim passage caused my spirit to soar, while supposedly uplifting passages from *The Book of Mormon* put me straight to sleep? And never was I sleepier than during my twice weekly religion class, which as a BYU student I was obligated to attend. Each would begin with the singing of a hymn, followed by an opening prayer, followed by a fifteen-minute-long roll call. The instructor would then bear his tearful testimony that the restored gospel is "true," and that Joseph Smith was a true prophet of God. Other religions of the world might be explored, but always "from an LDS point of view."

The only textbook I remember is something called the *Ricks Study Guide*, which posed such questions as, "Is it even possible that an uneducated country boy from upstate New York State could have penned *The Book of Mormon* without divine help?"

Being an undereducated country boy myself, I would say that Joseph Smith could very easily have written the book himself using reference materials readily available to him, such as the King James Bible and the Spaulding manuscript, a fictional work which spoke of prehistoric civilizations in North America. What's hard is writing a story that doesn't put the reader to sleep, and inventing names for characters that are original and not borrowed from somewhere else. Of course, that wouldn't have been the right answer. Not according to the Ricks Study Guide to *The Book of Mormon*.

Try as I might to regurgitate the correct answers, I didn't fare well in the class, barely pulling a C minus, which only served to drag down my grade point average. B's and C's weren't likely to get me into graduate school; however, I didn't much care. What good could come of making good grades at BYU? Thanks to Ernest Wilkinson's ongoing campaign to stamp out academic freedom, BYU's accreditation as an institution of higher learning was in jeopardy.

Was Wilkinson worried? Of course not. His overriding concern was that BYU not become a hotbed of liberalism or a haven for campus "radicals." Let Berkeley go to hell in a hand basket; Brigham Young would stand firm against the rising tides of change. All over campus, mirrors began to pop up.

Beneath each was a sign: HOW DO YOU LOOK? If you didn't look right, a "standards monitor" would suddenly appear to remind you that your hair was too long or your skirt too short. Appearances mattered; in particular they mattered to fat cat potential donors looking to contribute to a conservative enterprise. To all outward appearances, Brigham Young was the one college in America where you could send your youngster without having to worry he or she would be corrupted by some emerging social trend.

For those of us trapped *inside* the fortress, the picture wasn't quite so rosy.

"Brigham Young University is without doubt the most repressive environment anywhere outside the Soviet Union," declared Steve the Beatnik. "The teachers complain that my ideas are sophomoric and half-baked. Well, maybe so. But I say the so-called "ideas" expressed at BYU are overly baked. All the flavor is gone, like my mother's pot roast."

Most of us in English 318 understood what Steve was talking about, especially the part about the overcooked pot roast. We applauded the allusion. Encouraged, Steve pressed on. He declared how much he hated the recently completed Ernest L. Wilkinson Student Union Building, the architectural style of which he likened to a Soviet tenement.

"And have you ever noticed? No two chairs in the entire building face one another. What kind of a union building is it where it's impossible to carry on a conversation with another person?"

Soon as class let out, I made straight for the so-called "Wilk," where I discovered that Steve's observation was only slightly half-baked. A few chairs did face in the direction of other chairs; however, the people who occupied those chairs weren't talking to one another, but rather were staring vacantly into space like department store mannequins.

"Where are the thinkers?" I wrote in my diary that night. "Why don't they come out from their hiding places and speak up? I know they're out there; I hear them murmuring behind the scenes. We must unite! If those in power succeed in keeping us apart and rendering us mute, then one by one we'll be conquered."

Presently I was informed that Steve and his precious few allies were planning to launch a new literary magazine, one they described as "a journal of half-baked thinking." I volunteered to help, along with half a dozen like-minded English 318 enrollees. Dr. Larson lent moral support to the project, but cautioned us against being *too* creative. Although he was chairman of the creative writing program at BYU, Larson didn't have much pull with the powers that be. Only the year before, church authorities had attemptted to stop Provo City from staging Dr. Larson's religious play *The Redeemer*, citing the playwright's unconventional portrayal of Jesus. In 1959 he'd been relieved of his duties as editor of *Brigham Young University Studies*—again, because something he'd chosen to print had been deemed insufficiently conventional.

Aware that wrap-around sunglasses and a goatee might not be selling points, we dispatched assistant editor Susan Leotards to meet with university president Earl Sprockett, who had been holding down the fort while Ernest Wilkinson was away campaigning for a U.S. Senate seat. Unfortunately, Sprockett had been already been alerted by campus spies that plans were afoot to launch an offbeat publication, one that might address "controversial" issues of the day.

"I'm sorry," Sprockett told Susan, "but there is no room for controversy at this institution. And that was that for *The Half-Baked BYU Review*.

In spite of the fact I had nowhere to publish, I continued to write, and Dr. Larson took obvious pleasure in reading my words before the class. Then one day after the bell rang, he summoned me to his office and told me to take a seat. He asked what the folks back home in Carbondale thought of me.

I told him I had no idea. "At one time, I'd been considered a natural born leader, but now I have no followers. I have few friends. Even my own parents seem disappointed in how I've turned out."

"How do you think *I* feel?" responded Dr. Larson. "I've been here *seventeen years*—at BYU!"

Seventeen years. Dr. Larson had been at Brigham Young for almost as many years as I'd been alive. I could scarcely imagine a transgression in the pre-existence so grave as to warrant such a punishment.

"Have you given any thought as to what you'd like to do after you graduate?" he continued.

Not sure what he was driving at, I offered up the usual evasions. If I had learned anything at BYU, it was the necessity of *never* speaking one's mind. I was only halfway through my list of fictional career plans when he interrupted me.

"Richard, have you ever thought about applying for a teaching fellowship?"

"Are you offering me one?"

"Would you like one?"

"Well ..."

Larson buzzed the office of Dr. Bruce Clark, dean of the English Department, in whose American Literature class I had failed utterly to distinguish myself. I was such an unremarkable pupil, in fact, that Dr. Clark didn't at first recognize me.

"Bruce, this is Richard Menzies," declared Dr. Larson. "I think he's a bright boy."

"Menzies ... Menzies ..." Clark extended his right hand while scratching his head with the left.

"I was in your English 359 class," I explained.

"Oh, yes. I remember," he lied.

Dr. Clark returned to his office, not scratching his head now but shaking it. If first impressions counted for anything, my chances of landing a teaching fellowship were nil.

"I wouldn't worry about whatever grade you got in Dr. Clark's class," said Larson. "Grades aren't the most important thing. What's important is that you keep working. Keep *writing*. You *do* want to be a writer, don't you?"

"Well—yes. A writer is *exactly* what I want to be."

"Then stop apologizing. If you're going to be a writer, you need to project confidence! Don't worry about what others think. You're special! The person who wrote *this* (He waved my manuscript in front of my face.)—the person who wrote this is an *aristocrat*. So, from now on, I want you to *act* like one!"

CHAPTER TWENTY-ONE

SOUNDS OF SILENCE VS. SOUND OF MUSIC

So there I was. Still at BYU but with an ally in the English Department. I had a job offer of sorts, one that would keep me in school and out of Vietnam for the foreseeable future. I could earn a master's degree—maybe even a doctorate. I would become a teacher of creative writing and a writer—perhaps even the long hoped-for, oxymoronic "Mormon Hemingway." And even though I wasn't a returned missionary, perhaps I could forget that nigglesome doctrinal nonsense and embrace the culture into which I'd been born. In time I might come to love living in Provo—same as kidnap victims are wont to bond with their abductors. And even though I wasn't a returned missionary from a proper zip code, perhaps I could find a girl who loved me and only me. If not Mimsy Farmer, then perhaps someone closer to my own caste.

Doctor Larson had suggested that Susan Leotard and I might be a good match, she being the daughter of a gas station owner. Not a bad idea; unfortunately Susan had been "saving herself" for a missionary in the field. I mean, really, she was determined to wait for this guy.

Then, the result of a blind date arranged by Robbie's girlfriend Charly, I suddenly found myself keeping company with a young woman by the name of Molly Anna Prozack. Our first date found us sitting in a crowded movie theater, Molly clutching my hand tightly. The film we were about to see, she assured me, would lift me out of my silly funk forever!

The lights dimmed and the projector rolled. Up on the silver screen, Julie Andrews twirled in an alpine meadow, then burst into song. It was the famous opening scene of David Lean's *The Sound of Music*, a film Molly had already seen four times. Others in the audience had seen it dozens of times, and there were some who would go on to see it *hundreds* of times! Throughout Utah, *The Sound of Music* was being hailed as *The Greatest Story Ever Told*.

What was so great about it? Well, as a role model for young Mormon women, Maria Von Klapptrapp was perfect. Maria was pretty but not *too* pretty; she was a musically talented virgin who wore her skirts long and her hair short. Best of all, she was good with children—*lots* of children! As for Baron Von Klapptrapp, he was pretty much the prototypical authoritarian, never-at-home Mormon father.

I was the only person who walked out of the theater that night wearing a long face. Something about the relentlessly upbeat Von Klapptrapp singers had deepened my depression. Molly was confused. Even I was confused.

Back at Molly's apartment in University Village, Molly took a look at me and made a frowny face. "I think it's time you took Dr. Molly's foolproof psychological exam," she chirped. "Here, come lie down on my couch."

"Molly, I *am* lying on your couch," I said. "We've been lying here for almost an hour now."

"Okay, then stay where you are. I'll sit up and ask the questions, just like Sigmund Floyd."

"*Freud*," I corrected.

Molly told me to close my eyes and conjure up a mental image of a body of water. What sort of lake was it? Was it a pristine alpine lake ringed about by evergreens? Were there pretty birds perched on the branches? A speckled fawn grazing in the foreground? A little cottage beside the lake with a light in the window and tendrils of fragrant smoke rising from the chimney?

"No," I answered. "I see a brownish puddle swarming with biting insects. Overhead, the sun is a pale yellow disc, its warming rays blocked by a blanket of sulfurous smoke from the stacks of a nearby steel mill. In other words, I'm looking at Utah Lake."

"Whoa!" interrupted Molly. "There are no biting insects. And the sky is always blue. My goodness, you really *are* depressed!"

Molly announced she had just the cure for what ailed me. And I must confess, the treatment she had in mind certainly did me no harm. That is, not immediately.

For the next few days I wandered the campus in a daze, suffering from what I thought might be love sickness but which was later diagnosed as infectious mononucleosis—also known as "kissing disease." Molly Anna was looking a bit glassy-eyed as well; her roommates concluded she had fallen in love.

But was I in love with her? Well, why not? After all, I had come to BYU in hopes of snagging a girlfriend, and now I had snagged one. Unlike Scarlett and Miss Virginia Wilton, Molly wasn't a snob. Economically and socially, we two came from similar backgrounds, so there wasn't any chance I'd be receiving a parent-dictated Dear John letter any time soon. My lack of sophistication wasn't likely to be a problem; if anything, I was a bit brighter and a tad more sophisticated than Molly. My taste in art extended beyond Thomas Kinkade and I had seen more than just one movie—so she looked up to me and was careful never to say anything demeaning. And try as I might, I could find nothing the matter with her—that is, nothing that couldn't be fixed by another hot and heavy make-out session followed by 500 milligrams of penicillin.

CHAPTER TWENTY-TWO

I HAVE A DREAM

Molly Anna had begun phoning every night, wanting to spend ever more time with me. And whenever we were together, she was *on fire*—urging my hands onward, upward, downward. There was none of that phony propriety that had tainted my make-out sessions with Scarlett. No obligatory church meetings, no ritualistic roast beef dinners, no highfalutin lute and flute concerts and poetry readings. With Molly, I could do whatever I wanted, because whatever I wanted was the same thing *she* wanted. Anything I wanted her to become, she immediately became. Those who saw us together declared we were a perfect match and predicted that before long the two of us would be walking down the aisle or whatever it is they walk down or pass through inside the holy temple. A veil or something—symbolic entry to the other side. And if we should have actual intercourse before-hand—not to worry. "It's not as if the bishop is a gynecologist," said Molly.

So *why* wasn't I deliriously happy? I couldn't say. Whatever it was that was eating at me, it was now interfering with my sleep. Blessed Morpheus, why had he abandoned me?

Late one sleepless night, I turned to my roommate Robbie—who had just returned from a long, cold shower following a sweaty workout with his girlfriend Charly.

"Your problem is, you think too much," he said. "Thinking can get you into a lot of trouble—especially in a place like this. Why can't you just stop worrying and go with the flow? Stop kicking against the pricks, so to speak. And if you're thinking of dumping Molly, forget about it. The girl *adores* you! Charly tells me you're all she ever talks about."

"I just don't know, Robbie. There was a time in my life—last summer, for instance—when I thought that having a girl of my own would solve all my problems. But now I'm not so sure. To tell you the truth, I'm scared."

"Scared? Of what? Molly Anna?"

"Terrified. I'm afraid if I go to wherever it is she's leading me, there'll be no coming back."

"Oh, you can always come back. Hell, *I* came back."

"What are you talking about?"

Robbie drew a deep breath. "Have you ever wondered, brother, why it is your returned missionary roommate doesn't wear the funny underwear?"

"Temple garments? I haven't given it much thought. Personal choice?"

"Personal choice, my ass! I'm not entitled. I was *excommunicated*."

"You're kidding. For what?"

"Same thing you and Molly have been up to, except that I just happened to be in the mission field at the time. I succumbed to temptation and partook of the forbidden fruit. So now it's back to Fruit of the Loom."

"That is really shocking, Robbie."

"What's shocking about it? You think it never happens?"

"In *France*, sure. But Guatemala?"

"Doesn't matter where in the world they send you; temptation is everywhere—especially when you're trying to go about the Lord's business. Trust me, in some underdeveloped countries, plastic name tags are babe magnets."

"And so you got caught with your garments down...."

"Right. The mission president sent me home early. My parents were crushed, said they'd rather I'd come home in a pine box. I was hauled before a bishop's court, and they took away my temple recommend."

"And so here you are now a student at Brigham Young? If you're such a champion of free love, how come you're not at Berkeley?"

"*Because*—like I've been trying to tell you—once a Mormon, *always* a Mormon. Do you think it's easy being an outcast? An outsider? Trust me, there's no future in it."

"Perhaps. On the other hand, being on the outside looking in might not be the worst thing. Look, I've been doing a lot of reading lately. Do you realize how many of our greatest writers were outcasts?"

"But I have no intention of becoming a great writer," Robbie shot back. "I'm a business major, and after I graduate from BYU I'll marry Charly and become a junior executive in her father's Multilevel

Multivitamin Marketing venture. And in the fullness of time, I'll be head honcho: Mr. Multilevel Multivitamin Man himself."

"In spite of the fact you wear Jockey shorts?"

"Oh, I'll be sporting garment lines again by then. Have you not heard of the principle of repentance? I can change. We can *all* change. Even *you* can change, brother."

"I *am* changing," I said. "But not the way I'm supposed to. I'm afraid I'll never fit into the system."

"Well, maybe you won't have to. You say that you want to be a writer? Well, fine and dandy! But I'm going into business, and I'll be in need of connections. And what better place to make those connections than in church? And—speaking as someone who someday will rise to a position of authority—I feel duty-bound to warn you that rebellion is a dead end. I tried it and it didn't work."

So that was it. My friend Robbie the Bruce was just another of those semi-wayward Latter-day Saints who'd "gone through a phase." Soon enough he'd be back in the fold and moving upward via family connections and church contacts. Sure, he'd experience rapid weight gain and his hair would fall out, but he'd have a pretty wife, six adorable kids and a mini-castle in the suburbs. And honestly, what more in life could he ask for? An oak den or a pine box—those were his two options. Suddenly I felt sorry for him—even sorrier than I felt for myself.

My thoughts turned to my boyhood pal, Sven, recently returned from the New Zealand mission field. I remembered how pale and washed-out he looked the night he stood before the congregation to speak of his "fantastic" sojourn among the Kiwis. But his eyes didn't sparkle and his voice was oddly flat. Every trace of boyish exuberance was *gone*. Miraculously, Sven's girlfriend had waited for him, and within six weeks the pair had married in the temple. Shortly thereafter he enrolled in optometry school. Eventually he would become a bishop and spiritual advisor to his own band of unruly Mormon boys. As it was ordained in the beginning, so will it end.

Along came another Sunday, which I passed as usual wandering the mostly deserted streets of Provo. Had I been a coffee drinker at the time, and had there been such a thing in Provo as a coffeehouse, I might have spent the morning discussing poetry over a cup of java with Steve the Beatnik. Alas, there was no coffeehouse, and no Steve the Beatnik. Steve had gone missing—same as Dwight—shortly after being charged with disturbing the peace. Following the demise of *The Half-Baked Review*, he had resorted to reading his poems aloud to passersby on the quadrangle just outside the doors of the Wilkinson Student Center. He'd been hauled off to the Smoot Administrative Building and now all was quiet at the Wilk, save for the slurping of fourteen percent butterfat ice cream from The Creamery.

I made my way to Academy Square, pausing at the outdoor basketball court where I'd passed many a Sabbath driving the baseline against invisible opponents. But now my path to the basket was blocked by a large sign: SUNDAY PLAY PROHIBITED.

I continued down University Avenue to downtown, thence east along Center Street, which dead ends at the Utah State Mental Hospital. From a window on the second floor came the wailing of a soul in torment. Was it Dwight? Steve? Would it soon be *me*?

That night I had a most unusual dream—a dream so vivid that it jolted me awake. I dreamt I was back home in Carbondale, seated on a hardwood pew, surrounded by familiar faces, approving adults and companionable chums. Just like in the old days! As a special treat, Sister Brumwell announced that a visiting trio of elderly brethren would lead the congregation in singing the closing hymn. We were directed to open our hymnals to a particular page. She then cued the organist and raised her baton:

We shall overcome, we shall overcome

We shall overcome some day;

When by the light of a glorious dawn

We'll awake to find the crap is gone.

What? Hearing the word "crap" sung in a church setting was most unsettling. The congregation instantly fell silent; the organist's fingers froze in midair. Like a startled weasel, Orrin Snarr sprang from his upholstered seat and dashed to where the trio stood, their faces reflecting only mild puzzlement at all the commotion. Bishop Snarr directed their attention to the printed page, whereupon I checked my own hymnal. I was surprised to discover the trio had gotten it nearly right. The word was indeed "crap." However, they had left out an adjective, the prescribed lyric being "We'll awake to find the *original* crap is gone."

The three men studied their hymnals for a moment, then nodded in agreement. Without bothering to start anew from the top, they began where they had left off. Why start over when the song, for all intents and purposes, had already been sung?

When by the light of a glorious dawn

We'll awake to find the original crap is gone.

And with that they laid down their songbooks, stepped down from the dais, marched down the aisle and out the door.

Not very long afterward—no longer asleep but fully awake—I followed them out.

THE END

Also by Richard Menzies:

- *Passing Through: An Existential Journey Across America's Outback*

- *The Short, Short Hitchhiker (With Stanley Gurcze)*

www.ingramcontent.com/pod-product-compliance
Lightning Source LLC
Chambersburg PA
CBHW032042090426
42744CB00004B/92